New Perspectives on Black Studies

New Perspectives on Black Studies

EDITED BY
JOHN W. BLASSINGAME

University of Illinois Press
Urbana/Chicago/London

For those of my teachers who first taught me
there was no substitute for reason,
Myron Clemmons and David W. Bishop.

Preface

OVERWHELMED, as practically everyone else was, by the outpouring of interest in Black Studies, I began collecting material on the subject early in 1968. I was primarily interested at first in trying to clarify my own thinking on the subject. Hopefully, the essays in this collection will help others to make the process less painful than my own.

Fortunately, I had help from several people in clarifying my thoughts. Louis Harlan of the University of Maryland, C. Vann Woodward of Yale, William S. McFeeley of Mount Holyoke College, Oscar Bouise and James Welch of Xavier University, David W. Bishop of Fayetteville State University, and James Wood of Louisiana State University read and commented on an earlier draft of my essay, "Black Studies and the Role of the Historian." I also learned much from the reactions of the black students at Xavier, Louisiana State University, and Southern University to an oral presentation of the paper. Similarly, the criticisms of Andress Taylor of Federal City College and Otey Scruggs of Syracuse University at the December 1969 meeting of the American Historical Association made me much more aware of the complexities of the subject than I would have been otherwise. Mary F. Berry of the University of Maryland, Michael Winston, Olive Taylor, Lorraine A. Williams, and Letitia Brown of Howard University not only shared many of their ideas with me, but also suggested some of the essays included in this collection. Mrs. Dorothy Porter and Mr. James Johnson of the Negro Collection at Howard University gave invaluable assistance in my efforts to compile a bibliography on Black Studies.

My wife Teasie has remained cheerful in spite of my periodic frantic searches for "more relevant" essays and of having to endure my excitement and depression over each new version of the collection. Many of the strengths of the book are a result of her critical reading.

Table of Contents

Introduction

THE DEBATE over the place the Negro should occupy in American society has been raging, sometimes emotionally and sometimes dispassionately, since 1619. For centuries educational institutions have largely ignored the persons and issues involved in the debate. Ironically, as they seek to rectify past errors, American colleges and universities are confused over the proper response they should make. Many, however, are trying, by establishing Black Studies programs, to devote more attention to the role of black men in American society.

The process of establishing Black Studies is fraught with problems and frustrations. It has all happened so fast. Before 1968 the notion that a university student could earn a degree in Black Studies was almost unimaginable. Since then, scores of colleges have answered the insistent demands of black students by establishing a variety of Black Studies programs— often with precipitous speed. The racial provincialism of white scholars and institutions and the increasing number of black students in these institutions has led directly to the demands for Black Studies. The movement is also part of the general demand for "relevance" in education. Black and white students are demanding that colleges deal with life, its real options, dreams, problems, beauties, and ugliness.

Central to any discussion of Black Studies are the demands of the black students in predominantly white institutions. Obviously they are trying to increase their sense of pride and dignity and to destroy the myths which have distorted the image of the black man in their minds and in the minds of whites. Closely allied with this desire are the heavy pressures on the black student in predominantly white colleges. Accepting the myth that education liberalizes, in race as in other matters, the black student found, instead, all of the degrading assumptions and usages of the larger society enshrined in white academia. Treated as an untouchable by his white classmates, expected blindly to imitate everything white, fearful that he may follow the path of other educated blacks and abandon his people, and thrown into brutal academic competition with students who frequently are better prepared for it, the black student's life is understandably trying. Since whites have so rarely proved capable of respecting blacks, one reaction of the students is to reject everything white. In this context, only courses about blacks are "relevant," and only those courses taught by blacks and those programs controlled by blacks can "tell it like it is." (Many white students, disillusioned by the deception practiced on them by their parents and teachers, also subscribe to this view.) Feeling no desire to imitate white behavior in order to win white "acceptance" and rejecting the impersonality of the "multiversity," the black students demand separate social facilities as a refuge from whites. In their efforts to obtain these objectives, black students have frequently taken over administrative offices, called student strikes, presented "nonnegotiable demands," and sometimes used violence. Although their campaigns often disrupted campus activities, they were almost always brilliantly planned and executed.

The first black students at white colleges have urged administrators to abolish their usual admission standards in order to recruit more black high school graduates. The students argue, and rightly so, that the hellish cycle of inferior black education can be broken most easily at the college level—it will take too long to revitalize the public schools. At the same time, they are insisting that the white college acknowledge its own responsibility for discrimination against blacks in its admission procedures.

A number of people have raised serious questions about these new moves and especially "open admission" for blacks. First of all, they see such practices as extremely paternalistic and as a kind of reverse discrimination against qualified white students. Some black educators argue that lower admission standards are an insult to the black high school graduates. After all, so many white colleges have such low (or nonexistent) admission standards that anyone who has the fortitude to finish high school can gain admission to them. This, of course, is not true of most of the colleges where demands have been made for "open admissions." Many educators are also fearful that if scores of unprepared black students are thrown into competition with highly qualified white students at some of the nation's best colleges they will inevitably be frustrated. Even so, they feel that white colleges should make a concerted attempt to recruit more black students by emphasizing interviews and high school recommendations more heavily than test scores.

The black students have won their victories so quickly that they have not had time to ponder their meaning. Can victories won so easily indicate full acceptance by white academics of the new programs? Might not the white college's rapid capitulation to their demands indicate a lack of serious interest in the needs of black people and an insidious kind of paternalism?

Black Studies is so intimately related to contemporary problems and issues that it cannot be discussed purely in the abstract. It is embroiled, first of all, in campus politics. But if Black Studies is established merely to prevent campus disruption, the result may be a waste of time for students whose intellectual skills are desperately needed by the black community and the country at large. Second, Black Studies is a reflection of the contemporary efforts of blacks to define their relationship to white America. The widespread discussion of revolution, separation, and integration in the black community has forced many white scholars, out of a combined sense of guilt and a need to identify with "liberal" movements, to support the most intemperate demands of blacks. These whites, secure in their comforts and careers, want a kind of revolution that would not affect their security and would provide them with an interesting diversion. Others support separate, autonomous programs because they believe in segregation or because they see this step as a way of satisfying a few blacks without having to spend the massive sums of money needed to satisfy all blacks.

No aspect of Black Studies has caused more controversy than the demand of the black students for separate, autonomous programs controlled entirely by blacks. This is partially a reflection of the deep-seated distrust of white institutions by American blacks—they have been sold out so often by whites that they are no longer willing to entrust their destiny to any white man. Whites are too paternalistic and too few of them respect black men (Would you let your daughter marry one?), and too many of them are searching for relief from the terrible burden of guilt they bear, the students argue, for blacks to waste time either trying to convert or to save them. Separate dormitories, classrooms, and social facilities will permit blacks to work on common problems, to find psychological support in their fight against white racism, and to perfect the plans needed to save the black community. These objectives are so foreign to white students, and their life styles, dreams, behavior, and understanding of society are so different from Negroes that they would either be bewildered in classes with blacks or would slow the pace of the more advanced blacks. Separate, autonomous programs are a recognition of the uniqueness of black culture. Integration has failed. Negroes must withdraw into their own communities, strengthen them, and then obtain an equitable slice of the American pie. On the campus, the black students must withdraw into separate classrooms and social centers to rebuild their psyches and then rejoin the pluralistic society.

The opponents of segregated Black Studies programs believe that they represent the final step on the road to apartheid, the concept that every different race has a separate culture which calls for separate curricula and educational institutions. They contend that most blacks do not want racial separation and should not, in fact, struggle to achieve (or to maintain) it. Black Studies should represent an acknowledgment of the multiracial character of America and a recognition that Negroes have contributed to the formation of American society just as the Germans, Italians, English, and Hungarians have. If black or white students are to live effectively in such a society they must study in an interracial setting. Besides, Negroes need every opportunity they can get to learn the way that white men think if they are to compete successfully with them. By the same token, white students must have every opportunity to learn how blacks think if they are ever to understand or to respect them.

Most critics of separate facilities have simply asserted that any form of segregation, regardless of who demands it, is a retreat from the ideals of integration which so many people have fought for throughout American history. Even those who value "integration" less than these critics contend that separate facilities for black students at white colleges are self-defeating. It is unrealistic, they assert, for black students to build a comfortable all-black world within the white college.

The cynics among them argue that if the black students really wanted an all-black environment, they would have gone to an all-black college. They see no relationship between providing separate facilities for different nationality and religious groups and for blacks (as some administrators contend). While the other forms of separation are based on fundamental cultural, language, and religious differences, separation of black and white students is based solely on skin color. These critics believe that if Negroes are given "separate" facilities, inevitably they will become "unequal."

Many blacks argue that Black Studies must be a training ground for black liberation. Classes, therefore, would be forums for political indoctrination and the training of revolutionary cadres to organize the black masses. Black Studies must help to mold the oppressed in the Third World into a solid revolutionary phalanx to end white supremacy and white exploitation. The focus of this effort is on African culture and languages. The opponents of this approach contend that Black Studies is strictly an educational program for the dissemination of knowledge and the promotion of scholarship. They believe that it is impossible for predominantly white colleges, part of the oppressor's "establishment," *ever* to be agents in the establishment's destruction. One is dreaming if he believes otherwise. The opponents of the revolutionary approach criticize the proponents of unity of the Third World for stressing Swahili rather than Arabic, Portuguese, Japanese, or Chinese if they are interested in communication between the oppressed, the colonized, and the exploited colored peoples of the world.

Another controversial feature of Black Studies is the emphasis on community action programs. Many people argue that Black Studies should train leaders for the black community and devise ways to solve its problems. Opponents of this approach argue that it belongs more properly in Schools of Social Work, and Departments of Sociology and Urban Affairs. They express much less faith in the promises or the ability of predominantly white colleges to solve the problems of the black community. They fear that in this instance the American colleges' penchant for Madison Avenue promotionalism has led them to increase expectations in the black community without making the commitment of funds and personnel to fulfill these expectations. They also suspect that many of the middle-class black students, feeling guilty because they were not born poor, are seeking atonement for that sin by visiting the ghetto briefly and sharing vicariously the pain of poverty. In encouraging this flagellation, many colleges are perpetrating a cruel hoax on the black students by implying that blacks, through their own efforts can lift up the black community. However many tools these students acquire in community action programs, they will be no more than teaspoons to remove all the poison from the oceanic cesspool of American racism. The critics doubt the sincerity of colleges which are simply making promises to cool down the anger in the black communities which surround them. If a college is sincere, it can answer "yes" to several questions. Does it pay its black service employees a living wage? Has it planned adult education courses, job training centers, student-staffed nursery schools for working mothers, or extended the college health services to residents of the black community?

Realistically, any attempt to establish Black Studies is seriously hampered by the shortage of trained personnel. When only .78 of one per cent of all the Ph.D.'s awarded in 1968 went to blacks, it is obvious that most colleges will find it impossible to accede to the demands of the black students and appoint only blacks to teach black-oriented subjects. While the supply of trained blacks is severely limited, the demand for them is great. Academia is already fighting a losing battle to obtain blacks when they can get high-paying jobs in industry and government. The past neglect of Black Studies and discrimination against blacks has limited the number of scholars, black or white, in this field. When hundreds of colleges try to establish good programs simultaneously, the existing resources are spread so thin that many programs will inevitably be of little value.

Course content, objectives, and teaching strategies in Black Studies programs will be influenced by several factors. The limited training that some of the teachers have received, coupled with their insecurity about it and their desire to prove their blackness or possession of "Soul," will cause many of them to teach what is popular or currently "relevant." Frequently this will mean a glorification of the black experience and an interpretation of that experience that would serve contemporary efforts of "revolutionary" blacks. Is this the only way to build pride or a revolutionary ethic in black students? It can be argued that students will learn more about the contemporary world (and how to change it) from studying Uncle Toms, black villains, and militant blacks than from studying black revolutionaries exclusively. After all, these groups were and are part of the *reality* of the past and the present. Can any college course guarantee the formation of pride after the student has been subjected to so much racist propaganda in the public schools? Will the ephemeral or spurious sense of self-worth the black student gains from such courses survive his acquisition of knowledge about the complex and baffling facts of history? There is also an unconscious assumption by advocates of the approach which glorifies the black experience that the truth about the black experience verifies the racist's picture of blacks. Since they believe that blacks have been unimportant agents in American society, they feel they must be glorified. The advocates of this approach assume that the "achievements" of blacks cannot be subjected to critical analysis and still engender pride in blacks or the respect of whites. Is it not possible that a critical study of the black experience will produce criticism, ambivalence, and revulsion as well as pride? Will the sense of self-esteem necessarily be decreased because of the other feelings? In the end, and regardless of what teachers do, the student must determine his own emotional relationship to the black experience.

The essays in this collection have been compiled in an effort to answer some of the complex questions posed by Black Studies. Nathan Hare, Roger Fischer, June Jordan, Michelle Russell, and DeVere E. Pentony explain the rationale for Black Studies. They contend that such programs would help the Negro to form a clearer sense of his own worth and white men to accept him as a human being. They insist that such programs are essential in the formation of a black intelligentsia and efforts to improve the black community.

The essays in Part Two focus on some of the problems involved in the establishment of Black Studies programs. Kenneth Clark and Stephen Lythcott debate the advisability of establishing programs which exclude whites. Eldon Johnson, Jack J. Cardoso, Clark, Eugene Genovese, W. Arthur Lewis, and John Blassingame call for a more dispassionate approach to the whole question. They insist that whites as well as Negroes need to know more about the black experience, that black students should not try to establish apartheid at the universities, that educational institutions should maintain high standards in the programs and that they should inaugurate cooperative ventures with Negro colleges in this area.

The role of the historian, through sins of omission or commission, in fastening the unflattering twentieth-century stereotypes on the Negro is recognized by all of the contributors. Joanna Schneider, Robert Zangrando, and John Blassingame argue that the historian by his moral insensitivity or conscious efforts to support white supremacy has made the Negro the "invisible man" of American history. While Schneider and Zangrando support separate classes for black and white students taught by instructors of their own color, Blassingame contends that qualified teachers should be hired without regard to race. The debate among historians is roughly parallel to those in the other disciplines related to Black Studies. For instance, Catherine Stimpson maintains that since whites rarely understand black literature, only blacks can teach or serve as literary critics. Darwin Turner, on the other hand, insists that thoroughly prepared instructors, black or white, can teach Afro-American literature.

The appendix contains a Model Program in Afro-American Studies prepared by several scholars. Discussing the rationale, the objectives, and the courses which should be included in Black Studies, these scholars claim that their Model can be used as a point of departure for colleges which are planning or reviewing such programs.

The different ideologies represented in the essays and the seriousness of the contributors will, hopefully, create the atmosphere for a meaningful dialogue on Black Studies. The disagreements among the contributors accentuate many of the controversial aspects of the programs. Yet, in spite of their disagreements, many of the contributors agree on several essential points: Black Studies is a legitimate and long overdue intellectual enterprise; it should and will produce change in the attitudes of blacks and whites; it will lead to improvements in the black community and train more sophisticated leaders for it; and the program should stress scholarship and the solution of pressing social problems. The various positions taken by the essayists provide important new perspectives on Black Studies.

PART ONE

Definitions

What Should Be the Role of Afro-American Education in the Undergraduate Curriculum?

BY NATHAN HARE

A sociologist, Nathan Hare has taught at Howard University and San Francisco State College. He is the author of The Black Anglo-Saxons *(1965) and several articles. Hare contends that the education blacks receive at predominantly white colleges is largely irrelevant to them. Courses taught by blacks and from a black perspective would prepare the students to return to their own communities and solve the problems facing them. Colleges can no longer ignore the needs of the black community and the ego needs of black students.*

To SOLVE THE PROBLEMS of the black race, Afro-American education must produce persons capable of solving the problems of a contagious American society. To solve the problems of American society, Afro-Americans must first blackwash—revamp—the existing educational system and revolutionize America's youth—black, yellow, brown, and white.

A black education which is not revolutionary in the current day is both irrelevant and useless. To remain impartial in the educational arena is to allow the current partiality to whiteness to fester. Black education must be based on both ideological and pedagogical blackness. To implement a relevant black education we must overthrow and eliminate the bulk of cur-

Reprinted by permission from *Liberal Education* LV (March, 1969): 42–50.

rent college and school officials who are unable to move with tidal change and shift the traditional gears of a business-as-usual complex. The racism rampant in America's schools, white and Negro, must be blacked out.

On the positive plane, Afro-American education must activate and energize the black intelligentsia toward giving greater direction to the people of the black nation. Toward this end, black youths must be prepared for power in both community and nation—the present predicament and sense of powerlessness must be eradicated—and infused with ethnic confidence and a spirit of self-assertion. This will enable them to regenerate and reconstruct their own black communities, break the deadly grip of poverty, and build a productive black future. Not only does the current educational system fail to achieve those things; it viciously operates as an obstacle to black fulfilment and the elevation of blackness—which is why it must be eradicated.

In the beginning, American education, particularly on the college level, was highly private, restricted to the few who were wealthy enough to afford it. Such persons, as social theorist Thorstein Veblen observed in *The Theory of the Leisure Class,* were characterized by a peculiar mentality in which, owing to the necessity for displaying one's wealth, it was prestigious to be free from productive endeavor. Any work done could not be remunerative and preferably should be of no significant use to anybody, let alone oneself; to waste time and have the time to waste was the symbol of prestige. Their educational enterprise was accordingly characterized by a "liberal arts" approach where students learned a little about a lot of things and a lot about nothing. The leisure-class syndrome and its snobbish motivations developed a preoccupation with lofty gobbledygook and paraphernalia such as footnoting. Students might be compelled to labor in memorizing the idiomatic expressions and the verb conjugations of dead languages; or, more currently, languages which invariably fade from the student's memory and, while remembered, are useless in post-college life.

As middle-class aspirants began to emulate the leisure class, and education was largely socialized, the principle of exclusiveness was reinforced by the need to stem the flood of recruits to professional occupations. Hence the student might make A's and B's in all required courses only to fail the comprehensive exam or the language test, or might pass all academic requirements only to fail the bar exam because of political beliefs or color of skin. Education lost much of its capacity for vitalizing the mind and, since the end-products became more important than the process, eventually amounted to a routine assimilation of approved bodies of knowledge, a process which fails to inspire a black child of working-class origin.

I sometimes shock students into a realization of the shallowness of the American college scene by walking into a classroom and throwing out a concept, preferably with a German-sounding name, such as *"Zeitschaft"* (whether this is a word, I do not know) which I may claim to be a concept of a societal condition in which there is widespread feeling of normlessness. While students are busy copying down the term, I proceed to show how to measure the intensity of the *Zeitschaft* predicament. This is accomplished, I further instruct, by computing an Index of Facial Response. An Index of Facial Response (by now I am calling it the IFR score) is computed by: (1) observing a sample of persons over a period of time, passing or encountering one another on a given street corner during a given day; (2) charting the number of smiles exhibited by the individuals comprising the sample; then (3) dividing this by the square root of two.

While the students are furiously engaged in copying this down, virtually slobbering in anticipation of returning to their dormitories where they will ambivalently complain of the difficulty of the course (perhaps requesting their roommate's aid in calling out the material from memory), I step back and explain my desire to have the students see the board clearly, inasmuch as I had made it all up. I further state that I knew that they did not understand it (no more than I had) and that they are not being educated, in spite of what they are accustomed to believe, by merely memorizing a professor's fodder and regurgitating it on his test.

White students, it is true, are victims of the same condition, but it is doubly alien to the experience of black students who, moreover, are burdened by many other unconscious assumptions of white supremacy. Take the matter of the cultural imperialism which white ethnocentrism produces. A white anthropology professor may think nothing of dividing African tribes into "primitive" and "westernized," then point out that primitive tribes are more characterized by the matrilineal system, tracing ancestry through the mother instead of the father, while neglecting to point out that this could be a more accurate procedure.

The black student who first called my attention to this fact indicated that "you have to take the mother's word for it and sometimes she doesn't know herself." He swore that a boy in his Georgia bayou community came home one day and told his father happily that he was going to marry a girl—let us call her Pearlie Mae. His father said, "Son, I didn't know it would go that far. You can't marry Pearlie Mae; that's my daughter; she's your sister. Don't tell your mamma, now." The boy moped around, then broke down and told his mother what was wrong. "That's okay," his mother consoled, "you can marry Pearlie Mae. Don't tell your daddy but he ain't your father."

Sociology classes will discuss the merits of the Moynihan report on the Negro family, incognizant of the implications of Moynihan's own figures showing, for example, that for every 100 nonwhite males between ages 25 and 40 in New York City, there are 33 extra females. Somebody, of necessity, must carry a greater sexual burden than is rightfully his share, or a number of women will languish in induced celibacy. At the same time, the condition is being intensified by the disproportionate rates at which black males are dying in the Vietnam encounter, depleting the relative supply of eligible black males a few years hence. This cold demographic fact will lead to family disorganization and high rates of adultery, no matter how "moral" or "stable" (as social scientists say) black sexual codes might be.

Similarly, anthropology professors will subject black students to discussions of the family disorganization among Africans in Kenya, for example—impervious to the fact that much family strife is a product of the Christian missionaries' importation of an alien monogamy which, replacing the existing polygamy, evidently geared to the demography and socioeconomic needs of the people, displaced surplus wives (in order to "save" them) and thus produced family disorganization, which anthropologists get grants and trips abroad to "study."

Courses in European history will skip over the slave trade, while courses in American history will mention black persons only with reference to slavery and the myth that Lincoln's restricted Emancipation Proclamation freed all of them. Courses and textbooks in literature remain lily white. Many white students spurred by involvement in civil rights activities and the daily prominence of the black struggle in news coverage, are growing keenly aware of these curious omissions, but it is ever so much more painful when the student is black.

And yet they know so well that they must somehow wade through this white milieu in search of ratification for the "white rat race" (which is a chore for anybody). The chore is simply compounded by the fact that, psychologically and otherwise, it does not relate so well to what is crucial to the black student's life, inclining him in too many cases to be motivated to give up. He eventually comes to see it as essentially "a bad set."

This sense of defeatism and despair is reinforced and magnified by the models of failure surrounding him in the black community. On top of that, exposure to harsh measures of discrimination, past or present, provoke a feeling of suspicion out of which can develop a negative definition of certain phenomena which the white middle class employs for social acceptance, including cultural symbols of status; it might become derogatory, for example, to be seen spending much time with books. Under the prevailing college system, structured so that an individual succeeds best by conforming most to middle-class values, black students labor considerably less prepared to cope than are white students of suburban training and experience. They grow naturally and indelibly alienated. It might become more "in" to be pretty good at cards, for example, which only multiplies the probability of failure in the academic arena. The black student—covertly at first—rightfully begins to question the nature of standards impassionately dangled above his head as obstacles to the acquisition of the stamp "qualified."

I spoke recently at Yale University, where I had occasion to ponder the blank and (in a good many cases) open-mouthed stares of ignorance on faces in the predominantly white audience when I related how all white students given a test by a black colleague and me had fundamentally flunked, being unable to identify such commodities as hog maws, fried pies and butter role. The professor-collaborator, a "blood" (black man) and I had been impelled to concoct the test (at the risk of falling victims to the fallacy of *reductio ad absurdum*) after a ruckus between black students and white administrators at a predominantly white college over the choice of a professor for a course in "ancient black history." The administrators' choice was a young white fellow, armed with an Ivy League Ph.D. and much lauded publications in "learned journals." The black choice of black students (preferred also by many white students) bore no college credentials but probably knew as much about ancient black history as anybody you ever saw, having recently spent two years haunting the Schomburg Collection in New York. Contrarily, the white professor knew little or nothing about the subject under scrutiny, he was quick to admit, but continued to cry out with strong emotion that he was "qualified." The black students who sought to break up his class could not understand why the administration would present a white man admitting his ignorance to teach a course while rejecting the "qualified black man."

Later, it occurred to me that a black historian seeking publication in learned journals is placed in the rather precarious and unfair position of having to document his work (when writing aggressively against the slavery era) with references from the writings and records kept by a slavemaster society in which black persons were restricted by law and custom from the power of the written word.

While a graduate student in sociology at the University of Chicago, I ran afoul of academia's dictates of copious footnoting, fleetingly scanning library shelves for instant references from unread books to win high marks and influence professors with padded documentation. (A Harvard administrator in the audience at Yale assured me that I did not invent that vulgar practice.) Even so, it was for me excusable because, unlike my professors who were unable to tell me the identity of "The Four Tops," I was "culturally deprived." I acquired the Ph.D. without gross dishonor, and that appears sometimes now to count in the minds of others more than all the good and bad things I have ever done.

My contempt grew stronger, in any case, as I discovered the footnoting cliques in references used to buttress white theorizing on the black race. Not only did I detect mutual-quoting affairs; I noted that a professor (as many did) might suggest hypotheses to thesis students who then graciously used some of the professor's work for references, only in turn to be used by the professor to document a larger theory based on the hypotheses of the several students. I learned further, while poring over learned journals, that the motivation behind the footnoted expressions of gratitude to wealthy foundations and colleagues was not gratitude alone. Nay, the fact that a top-rate foundation has backed a piece of research gives it the boost of prestige. The scholarly custom of sending a manuscript around to sundry colleagues reaps the insinuation that the colleagues named have given it the stamp of approval. This "dirty knowledge" (as one of my professors called it) gave me, as a faltering black student from a rural district in Oklahoma, a new kind of confidence.

Many experiences, which can turn him either on or off, confront the black college student in the typical white college classroom. For example, he must sit silently bemused while his eminent sociology professor reports, solemnly but proudly, that his surveys show that there will be no riots in Chicago because, as one suggested early last September, only seven per cent of Negroes surveyed say they definitely approve of riots. A black student might not realize that such a professor, like his peers at large, is suffering from the bias of democracy's myth of majority-rule, but the calculator in his brain might quickly register 70,000 blacks—as he longs for a bourbon on the rocks—and wonders how many Negroes his professor believes sufficient to start a riot. The professor himself may later have stood perplexed when rioting broke out in Chicago on the heels of Martin Luther King's assassination, but he is not likely to alter his methods or standards of "scholarly excellence" which he requires his black students to digest.

Early in his educational career, the black student encounters the subordinating slap of white supremacy. Modes of communication, for instance, compel him to lose his "in-group dialect" and imitate the snarls and twangs of the white race. "There" becomes "thear"; "nine," "nigh-yun"; "law," "lower," and so on. Verbal facility is frankly presented to the black student as the salient ingredient for admission to college, although I know young black men with more verbal facility than I will ever have who have either flunked out or dropped out of school.

Beyond this, the black student instinctively, if only faintly, is repelled by the fact that foreign languages required are exclusively of white European origin, though oriental languages may be offered as electives. This in spite of the fact that Chinese is spoken by more individuals than any other language in the world and Swahili, an African language, competes very favorably with German. This is just one of the examples of white snobbishness lurking behind the criteria of excellence which, however, is not entirely a product of racism alone. Running through its history is another strain of a fundamentally different sort, though it too is racial, by coincidence, in its consequences.

Black students who wail about the absence of blackness in white college education, therefore, are not trying to destroy American education so much as trying desperately to renovate it to permit their meaningful participation. Their compensatory response to black exclusion has taken a separatist flavor, for the most part on the surface; but it may seem ironic to those who misunderstand them that, in the name of black nationalism, calling for the presence of more black students and professors, they actually are bringing about more desegregation of white colleges than ever there was before.

The name of the game is the elevation of a people by means of one important escalator—college education. Separatism and integrationism are possible approaches to that end; they lose their effectiveness when, swayed by dogmatic traces of absolutism, they become full ends in themselves. It will be an irony of recorded history, as I have written elsewhere, that "integration" was used in the second half of this century to hold the black race down just as segregation was so instituted in the first half.

Black students now seem to feel that integration, particularly in the token way in which it has been practiced up to now and the neo-tokenist manner now emerging, elevates individual members of the group but paradoxically, in plucking many of the strongest members from the group while failing to alter the lot of the group as a whole, weakens the collective thrust which the group might otherwise muster. Increasingly, black students are turning their backs on the old tendency for Negro college graduates to seek to escape from the black community instead of returning to help build it. This new mood is born of a greater awareness of the glories of their own past as a people, an image they now wish to convey also to others. Hence the clamor for more "black courses" and courses taught *from a black perspective* (or "dark" courses, as I overheard one white colleague tell another—later translated by a sociology professor into "color-compatible" courses).

Black studies must be taught from a black perspective. The spirit of blackness must pervade black education. Many white professors—and consequently, of course, professors at Negro colleges—are beginning to dust off old race relations and Negro history courses and call them black. These are collected, usually remaining scattered under the control of existing—frequently racist—departmental chairmen. Such programs are not black studies; they are Negro studies or polka-dot studies. Nor is the blackening of existing white courses or white-oriented courses alone enough. Black education must be based on both ideological and pedagogical blackness.

Moreover, black studies may be divided into two basic phases: the expressive and the pragmatic-positivistic. The expressive phase is therapeutic (revitalizing the collective ego via courses in culture and history), while the pragmatic-positivistic stage is utilitarian (providing skills with which to bring about the change desired in one's life circumstances). Even those who recognize the value of black studies in the expressive sense, do not realize that distinction and seek to keep us bogged down in the areas of art and religion and history. We must not become so preoccupied with history that we neglect to act to make our current history and eventual future.

Afro-American education must also move into the scientific realm. Many opponents of black studies claim that science is "pure" and that there is no such thing as black science. Even if science is pure, which is debatable, the teaching of science is not. One might choose to focus on atomic weapons of destruction or on chemicals for rat extermination, relevant to reconstructing the black community. Even mathematics, for example: instead of reading problems referring to stocks and bonds, which we may mistake for mules and cattle, the problem might ask, "If you loot one store and burn two, how many do you have left?" While this example might be improved, it illustrates the kind of content which might whet the enthusiasm of the "ghetto" child.

Black education is black-community centered. At the least, the educational process must involve the black community, transforming the community while educating and training the black student. For example, students in a course in black history—let alone black politics or black economics—might be required to put on panel discussions for younger children in church basements. A course in black education would contain tutorial assignments. A class project for the black history class might be the formation of a black history club; a class in community organization could form civic clubs, while individual students served apprenticeships under community organizers. Students in black journalism, black economics (business), black education (teachers), black politics or what not, could do the same.

This would tend to increase the commitment of black students to the community while simultaneously permitting them to "learn to do by doing." At the same time, their mere presence in the community would provide role models not generally available to black youths. Thus education is made relevant to the student and his community while the community is, so to speak, made relevant to education.

Aside from the matter of intensified motivation (and increased commitment to the struggle to build the black community), students who have mastered even a smattering of black studies courses would be advantaged in their post-college work in the black community. They would be armed with early involvement and experience in the community superior to that of professionals not so educated. To develop this key component of community involvement, it is necessary to inspire and sustain a sense of collective destiny as a people and a consciousness of the value of education in a technological society. Skills are needed for success in any endeavor whether it be constructive or destructive. Pragmatism can be either positive or negative, depending on the needs of the black community at a given time and place. A cultural base, cemented by the expressive component of the black studies program and acting as a leverage for other aspects of black ego development and academic unity, would provide the sense of pastness or collective black destiny valuable as a springboard to a new future.

In the effort to make education "relevant" to the black community—and by indirection, to the white community—the communities themselves may be transformed, each in its own way, and, so to speak, made relevant to a bona fide education. Thus black student endeavors, if successful, might not only bring about a kind of black renaissance; they could possibly wield an impact on the entire cemetery of American education.

Ghetto and Gown:
The Birth of Black Studies

BY ROGER A. FISCHER

Roger Fischer received his Ph.D. from Tulane University and has written several significant articles on black history. He has taught at Southern University, Sam Houston State College, the University of Southwestern Louisiana, and currently at Southwest Missouri State College. Viewing the initial disappointments of black students at white colleges and their revolt against paternalism and the denial of their identity, Fischer chronicles the successful efforts of small cadres of blacks to create Black Studies programs. Once the legitimacy (often for political reasons) of Black Studies was accepted, the students could not agree with traditional academics about its meaning, the autonomy blacks were to have, or the relationship of whites to the programs. He argues that the reality of the situation will force students to drop many of their separatist demands.

UNLIKE MOST academic programs, black studies was not born in a faculty senate chamber or in a dean's conference room, or even on a college campus. It all began more than a decade ago at those Southern lunch counters and deserted bus stops where black people finally rose in rebellion against nearly three and a half centuries of second-class citizenship.

Northern college campuses soon became hotbeds of sympathy for the "movement" and in the process discovered embarrassing inconsistencies between their libertarian beliefs and their lily-white student bodies. All too often, black enrollment was limited to a star basketball player or two and a few local

Reprinted by permission from *Current History* 57 (November, 1969): 290–94, 299–300.

16

Negroes who showed up for classes, then obligingly disappeared when it was time for social activities. Finally, while the state universities of Mississippi and Alabama made their stand for segregation by massive resistance and redneck rhetoric "in the schoolhouse door," many of the better Northern schools began to fulfill a commitment to racial equality by earnestly recruiting black students without regard to their prowess at broken-field running or the zone defense.

These young black men and women undoubtedly went to college with naively high expectations. If Negroes since Booker T. Washington have regarded higher education as the key to opportunity, surely the prestigious Northern universities were the path to the promised land. Negro students were looking for the American dream, but found instead the bitter disillusionment of hopeless alienation. Some whites literally smothered them with paternalism. As one proud black man remembered his two years at Yale, he had been "the chosen one on whom all the benefits of a guilt complex could be bestowed—a kind of little tan Orphan Annie befriended by a great white Daddy Warbucks." Other whites tried to destroy racial differences by ignoring them. An eminent historian rhapsodized in his introduction to a study of slavery, "Negroes are, after all, only white men with black skins, nothing more, nothing less." In short, the white university unwittingly tried to transform its black students into what Lerone Bennett, Jr., has described as "Orwellian non-persons" by failing to come to terms with their blackness.

The identity crisis of the black students was compounded by the Anglo-Saxon orientation of their studies. American literature courses meandered from Michael Wigglesworth to J. D. Salinger without acknowledging the poems of Lawrence Dunbar or the novels of James Baldwin. Music professors blandly attributed the origins of jazz to Paul Whiteman. Few dramatics courses interrupted their readings of the hallowed classics to pay any attention to Lorraine Hansberry's brilliant *Raisin in the Sun*. All too often, the only Negroes encountered in studies of American culture were little Topsy, Uncle Remus, and those docile darkies of *Green Pastures,* Sambo stereotypes created by white writers for white readers.

United States history courses ignored the African heritage so completely that it seemed to Lerone Bennett as if "black Americans appear suddenly by a process of spontaneous generation." Negroes merited attention in American history surveys only when they were making trouble or when white agitators were doing so on their behalf. Ten Jeffersonians arrested under the Alien and Sedition decrees often received as much time as and more sympathy than four million enslaved blacks. Instructors spent weeks discussing the white immigrant ghettos of the nineteenth century, then ignored Harlem, Hough, and Watts altogether.

Stripped of their identities as black people and forced into a curriculum that denied their heritage by an unconscious conspiracy of silence, black students found themselves completely, irreconcilably alienated within the ivy-covered confines of the white universities. Integration seemed to lead only to invisibility and those tempted to try it were haunted by fears that they might become, as Dartmouth's F. Woody Lee put it, "little more in the eyes of many whites than a genteel nigger— a showcase coon." Rebellion seemed the only answer, and black students eagerly embraced the heady new doctrines of black consciousness. From Malcolm X they discovered the brotherhood of all blacks and the essential dignity of the black identity. From Stokely Carmichael and H. Rap Brown they learned how to transform Malcolm's teachings into the political activism of Black Power. And so they rebelled, in part against the racism of the white university system, but primarily against their own false prophets who had deluded them with hair straighteners and colored country clubs and Urban League brotherhood week banquets.

The wave of campus confrontations that began at the Berkeley campus of the University of California in 1964 was essentially a white phenomenon, but it provided watchful black militants with an excellent practical education in the tactics of disruption. From such white radicals as Mario Savio, they learned that a great university could be literally immobilized by boycotts, sit-ins, and the "liberation" of administration buildings. They discovered the awesome secret of student power, that the university was pathetically vulnerable to the pressures that could be brought to bear upon it by a relatively small cadre of well organized, deeply dedicated student revolutionaries. Blacks began to organize, and soon groups known by such titles as the United Black Students, the Association of African and Afro-American Students, the Onyx Society, the Soul Students Advisory Council, and the Black Students Union appeared on campus after campus.

The names may have differed, but the common goal of these organizations was the "de-honkification" of the universities. To achieve that result, these black student unions issued a series of demands, among them the hiring of more black professors and the enrollment of more black students through recruiting, scholarships, and relaxed admissions standards. Specific demands varied greatly, including moratoriums on failing grades, blanket subsidies for minority students, and a school holiday on the birthday of Malcolm X. But one demand was virtually universal and led nearly every list of priorities. It called for the creation of programs in black studies.

The idea was wholeheartedly embraced by many beleaguered administrations and faculties. Universities where tranquillity still reigned joined in the rush to establish black studies programs to head off future trouble. Everybody, it seemed, favored black studies in the abstract. The problems began on many campuses when the militants and the Establishment sat down together to iron out specific details and discovered that neither group had the slightest notion what the other really meant by "black studies." For the past two years, the development of black studies as an academic discipline has been stalled by this communications barrier. Unless one faction capitulates completely or both can agree on a common definition, black studies may be bogged down indefinitely.

Academic traditionalists, including most scholars and nearly all administrators, think of black studies as the body of subject matter relating to the Negro experience in Africa and the New World. Within their frame of reference, a curriculum in black studies would consist of such courses as African and American Negro history, tribal anthropology, the politics and sociology of ethnic minorities and Negro music, art, literature and theater. They would most probably be grouped together in an interdisciplinary "area studies" program, with supervision divided among a coordinating committee, the participating departments and the administration. These courses would be taught by professors, white or black, with the proper academic credentials, and would be open to all eligible students. In defining black studies in this manner, traditionalists are merely following hallowed academic practices. Courses have always been organized into disciplines by the nature of their subject matter. Control has invariably rested within the chain of command which comprises the administrative hierarchy. Possession or pursuit of the doctorate, not skin color, has long been the yardstick of serious scholarly intent.

These criteria, however important they may be to the maintenance of academic excellence, are regarded by many militant Negroes as irrelevant, possibly dangerous, obstacles to their pursuit of a black studies program as they envision it. They have not yet developed a common blueprint for the operational mechanics of a black studies program tailored to their tastes, although an ambitious project in that direction has been started by Vincent Harding at the Institute for the Black World in Atlanta. Most militants see black studies not as a labyrinth of curriculum committees and degree requirements, but as a collegiate training ground with a single over-riding purpose, the advancement of the black revolution in every facet of American life.

As Cornell's Harry Edwards has noted, "The time is gone for black cats to flee to Baldwin Hills and eat pickles and hors d'oeuvres and watch the riots on color TV." According to Nathan Hare, deposed black studies director at San Francisco State College, "black today is revolutionary and nationalistic. A black studies program which is not revolutionary and nationalistic is, accordingly, quite profoundly irrelevant." In keeping with the activist definition, a meaningful black studies program must train black students to organize the urban ghettos and the black-belt South, to utilize the tactics of civil disobedience against racial discrimination, and to guide their brothers and sisters who never got to college toward greater social, economic and political opportunities.

Embittered by the oppressions of the past and impatient to undertake the reconstruction of the future, these black militants hold very little reverence for traditional academic niceties. Lectures on such esoteric topics as "the social dynamics of a fifteenth-century West African agricultural village" or "Camille Thierry, free Negro poet in Paris" may indeed warm the cockles of the scholastic heart, but they seem rather pointless to those whose daily lives have been endless struggles against ghetto rodents or "white only" restrooms. Even topics much more pertinent to current realities have been dismissed by many activists as meaningless. Commenting on Edward Greenberg's course on "The Politics of Race" in the black studies program at Stanford University, one Negro student complained, "Greenberg tells us the blacks haven't gotten anyplace politically. . . . Hell, we know that. What I want to know is where we can go from here, and how."

Complaining about the Establishment's concepts on curriculum, Cornell's Bill Osby lamented, "They will simply let us study black history and wear *dashikis* while we get ready to work for Xerox or IBM." Black ideas on curriculum vary widely. Nathan Hare favors a "comprehensive, integrated body of interdisciplinary courses" emphasizing the "black perspective," including economics, science and mathematics. "Black mathematics," as Hare envisions it, "would not be saturated with middle-class referents such as stocks and bonds" and a course in "black biochemistry" might study such topics as rat control. Other black studies architects advocate more limited programs based upon the black experience in social sciences and the arts. Many activists demand a curriculum which reflects their revolutionary ideology. They favor such courses as San Francisco State's "Sociology of Black Oppression," in which instructor Jerry Vernado wrote out the formula for napalm so that his students could "pour it on a piece of meat or on the police or somebody and see exactly how it works."

If many black militants find conventional ideas on curriculum annoyingly irrelevant, they regard the traditional "power structure" of the university as the ultimate enemy. If absolute sovereignty over black studies rests with the deans and the trustees, Negroes fear that these programs will most probably be systematically emasculated of any productive value they might otherwise engender. Overwhelmingly white, middle-class, middle-aged and politically "safe," college administrators and trustees have come to personify the hated white Establishment to many campus blacks. This suspicion has led to demands for "autonomy," or black control over black studies programs.

Proposals on how autonomous status can be attained are varied, including such ambitious schemes as totally separate colleges for black studies within the university system, with independent governing boards and budgets. Most often, however, proponents of autonomy advocate separate departments of black studies with black student power over curriculum and the hiring and firing of faculty. This dispute has been a volatile one, for militants and administrators know well that the nature and philosophy of any academic program is largely determined by those who possess the ultimate control over it.

The most explosive issue of all has been the question of white participation in black studies. Directly related to the bitter integrationist-separatist controversy now ripping apart the delicate unity of the "movement" itself, black militant demands for the exclusion of white professors and students have alienated many Negroes and virtually all of the white academic community. Separatists argue that no white scholar, however illustrious his learned degrees and publications, can truly understand the black experience. As Johnie Scott, a Stanford University senior from Watts, expressed it, "No white man can talk about Rap Brown or Stokely Carmichael."

Separatists object to the presence of white students in black studies courses for a variety of reasons. Some of the more paranoid blacks have expressed the fear that whites would take advantage of the knowledge they gained to keep on exploiting the blacks. Others feel that the presence of whites retards open discussion. A black student at Oakland's Merritt College, urging a lone white to leave a class in black philosophy, pointed out, "So long as this white boy is in this class, we're going to be talking elliptically, all around and over the subject, but no one is really going to be saying anything."

A few schools have apparently surrendered to the new apartheid. At Merritt College, black instructors reportedly prevent white students from attending some of the 15 courses in their black studies program. Officials at other schools have allegedly ignored incidents in which whites have been ejected from classes by black student vigilantes. Antioch College gained nationwide notoriety by summarily excluding white students from its black studies institute, a policy which the United States Office of Education regarded as a violation of Title VI of the Civil Rights Act. Faced with the loss of federal funds, Antioch administrators defended their actions by arguing that admission to the program was based not on race but on its "relevance" to the needs and experience of the students, a subterfuge hauntingly reminiscent of the "grandfather clause" of another generation.

The Antioch situation is by no means commonplace, for nearly all college administrations have opposed institutional color lines and most Negroes reject separatism emphatically. As integrationist Negro spokesman Roy Wilkins has pointed out, "We have suffered too many heartaches and shed too much blood in fighting the evil of racial segregation to return to the lonely and dispiriting confines of its demeaning prison." Negro psychologist Kenneth Clark has stated that to encourage separatism "is to reinforce the Negro's inability to compete with the whites for the real power of the real world." Even Nathan Hare, an outspoken black militant, has remarked, "We think that separatism is often a pretext to evade acting in a revolutionary fashion now."

Even so, the Antioch controversy symbolizes too well the current dilemma of black studies. If it is ever going to develop into a meaningful academic discipline, traditionalists and black militants must somehow reach understandings on such basic issues as curriculum, control, and interracial participation. Accommodation will probably be difficult to achieve, for the rhetoric of revolution is seldom conducive to the realities of compromise. If confrontation is allowed to escalate beyond the point where reasonable debate remains possible, black studies will be the inevitable victim. The militants have been successful with the strategy of limited disruption, but they lack the power to immobilize most universities completely and even the most timorous trustees and administrators unquestionably have their breaking points. Every indication points to a rising tide of social reaction, to a climate in which repression would be welcomed by regents, legislators and a public which remembers too vividly the guns of Cornell. If reaction and repression ever become the order of the day, black studies will surely die the death of a sacrificial lamb.

It is most unlikely that many colleges will permit the militants to define the curriculum in terms of the philosophy of black revolution. To grant any ideology such privileged status would be a gross violation of the traditional concept of the university as a laissez-faire marketplace for the free exchange of ideas. Moreover, if most regents, administrators and legislators were given to promoting special treatment for any political philosophy, it most assuredly would not be Black Power. Few members of the Establishment would look fondly upon a black mathematics course in which, as Nathan Hare has suggested, the instructor might ask, "If you loot one store and burn two, how many do you have left?" It seems equally unlikely that black autonomy will be taken very seriously by most college administrations. Most regents and administrators believe that their surrender of control would lead to out-and-out anarchy. Few of them, needless to say, are anarchists.

The militants must also abandon the notion that white students and professors should be excluded from participation in black studies programs. This latter-day apartheid is legally questionable and morally indefensible. Moreover, separatism could well prove suicidal to the black studies program. If "white racism" is the greatest single obstacle to black aspirations, as the Kerner Commission has alleged, then white students would be the most logical beneficiaries of black studies. At the very least, their presence in the classes would add the element of interracial dialogue. Black studies programs also need qualified white professors, for such programs will need all of the academic talent they can muster to survive their infancy and justify their existence as a discipline.

White scholars have contributed substantially to black studies in the past. It would be impossible, for example, to imagine a course on slavery which neglected the writings of Kenneth Stampp, Stanley Elkins and Eugene Genovese or a study of segregation which ignored the works of Gunnar Myrdal, John Dollard and C. Vann Woodward. It would be tragic if the Myrdals and Woodwards of the future were forced to detour into other disciplines because black studies discouraged them with signs saying, in effect, "No Irish Need Apply."

Compromise should not come, however, completely on traditionalist terms. The proposals of the black militants may be impractical and in some cases academically unsound, but they convey an urgency and an immediacy so often missing in the Ivory Tower. Autonomy may be unrealistic, but black students certainly deserve a meaningful voice in determining the faculty and curriculum of black studies programs. Above all, the courses must attempt to meet contemporary needs. As the Stanford student pointed out, "What I want to know is where we can go from here, and how." Nathan Hare's concept of a black science course to study rat control is excellent and should be expanded into other areas. Black economics should study welfare survival in the ghetto and the feasibility of boy-cotting merchants guilty of discriminatory hiring practices. Black political science must teach its students to organize the ghetto and the bottomlands, to elect black officials and apply maximum pressure on white politicians. The possibilities are virtually endless.

If honest compromise is possible, the Establishment must remain rigid in defense of its academic integrity, but it must also allow enormous flexibility to avoid smothering promising innovations. It must remember that a university which buries its problems in the name of tranquillity has already abandoned its place in a free society. Black militants must realize that the failure of black studies might mean a return to the silent racism of college life as it was a decade ago. Compromise will undoubtedly demand twice the wisdom of Solomon and three times the patience of Job, but it must be achieved. The alternatives are frightening.

Black Studies: Bringing Back the Person

BY JUNE JORDAN

A poet-teacher-writer, June Jordan has participated in the SEEK program at the City College of New York and edited an anthology of poetry, Soul Script. *Jordan questions the value of traditional American education for blacks. Rather than liberate, it enslaves the black student. It allows the black student to define himself in white terms only. According to Jordan, the black student looks for the humane values of love and cooperation, while the educational establishment is dedicated to violence and exploitation. The universities can only help black students to find out who they are through the establishment of Black Studies. Jordan contends that the universities must not only change their curriculums, they must also establish Black Studies programs controlled by blacks and revise their admission policies so that more black students can attend them. And while blacks must become competent architects or engineers, they must also learn about themselves in Black Studies programs. A black can no longer become just a doctor, he must, according to Jordan, become a black doctor, conscious of the pain and beauty of blackness.*

All my life I had been looking for something, and everywhere I turned someone tried to tell me what it was. I accepted their answers too, though they were often in contradiction and even self-contradictory. I was naive. I was looking for myself and asking everyone except myself questions which I, and only I, could answer.

Ralph Ellison, Invisible Man

Reprinted by permission from *Evergreen Review,* October, 1969, pp. 39–41, 71–72.

BODY AND SOUL, Black America reveals the extreme questions of contemporary life, questions of freedom and identity: *How can I be who I am?*

We lead the world stubbornly down the road to Damascus knowing, as we do, that this time we must name our god. This time, gods will grow from the graveyard and the groin of our experience. There will be no skyborne imagery, no holy labels slapped around our wrists. Now we arise, alert, determining, and new among ourselves. I am no longer alone. We move into community of moment. We will choose. But not as we were chosen, weighed and measured, pinched, bent backwards, under heel; not as we were named: by forced dispersal of the seed, by burial of history, by crippling individuality that led the rulers into crimes of dollar blood.

We, we know the individuality that isolates the man from other men, the either/or, the lonely-one that leads the flesh to clothing, jewelry, and land, the solitude of sight that separates the people from the people, flesh from flesh, that jams material between the spirit and the spirit. We have suffered witness to these pitiful, and murdering, masquerade extensions of the self.

Instead, we choose a real, a living enlargement of our only life. We choose community: Black America, in white. Here we began like objects chosen by the blind. And it is here that we see fit to continue—as subjects of human community. We will to bring back the person, alive and sacrosanct; we mean to rescue the person from the amorality of time and science.

History prepares the poor, the victims of unnecessary injustice, to spit at tradition, to blow up the laboratories, to despise all knowledge recklessly loosened from the celebration of all human life.

And still, it lies there, the university campus, frequently green, and signifying power: power to the people who feed their egos on the grass, inside the gates.

Black American history prepares black students to seize possibilities of power even while they tremble about purpose. *Efficiency, competence:* black students know the deadly, neutral definition of these words. There seldom has been a more efficient system for profiteering, through human debasement, than the plantations of a while ago. Today, the whole world sits, as quietly scared as it can sit, afraid that tomorrow America may direct its efficiency and competence toward another forest for defoliation, or clean-cut laser-beam extermination.

Black American history prepares black people to believe that true history is hidden and destroyed, or that history results from a logical bundling of lies that mutilate and kill. We have been prepared, by our American experience, to believe that civilization festers between opposite poles of plunder and pain. And still the university waits, unavoidable at the end of compulsory education, to assure the undisturbed perpetuity of this civilization.

We have learned to suspect and to beware the culture belied by phrases such as "the two-car family," or "job security," or "the Department of Defense," or "law and order."

We do not deride the fears of prospering white America. A nation of violence and private property has every reason to dread the violated and the deprived. Its history drives the violated into violence, and one of these days violence will literally signal the end of violence as a means. We are among those who have been violated into violence.

Black American experience staggers away from the resurrecting lord of love. In his place, we must examine the life, through death, of Bigger Thomas. We know he was not paranoid. Crazy, yes. Paranoid, no. We know how his sanity died, and who his well-educated executioners were. And the black student of his life brims hatred for the hateful choice allowed to Bigger Thomas, hatred for an efficiency that cancels, equally, the humanity of the oppressed and the oppressor. Even so, we confront a continuing tyranny that means Bigger Thomas may yet symbolize the method of our liberation into human community.

How will the American university teach otherwise? One favorite university precept is that of reasonable discourse. We ask, when Bigger Thomas stood there, black-male-in-white-girl's-bedroom, what did reasonable discourse offer to him? Who would have listened to his explanation of himself next to the drunken white woman, on her bed?

In America, the traditional routes to black identity have hardly been normal. Suicide (disappearance by imitation, armed revolt), and exemplary moral courage: none of these is normal.

And, if we consider humankind, if we consider the origins of human society, we realize that in America the traditional routes to white identity have not been normal, either. Identity of person has been pursued through the acquisition of material clues admittedly irrelevant to the achievement of happiness. Identity has been secured among watery objects ceaselessly changing value. Worse, the marketplace has vanquished the workable concept of homeground or, as children say in their games: home-safe.

But Black America has striven toward human community even within the original situation that opposed its development, the situation of slavery. Often enough, at the expense of conceivably better working circumstances, those enslaved pleaded not to be sold away from the extended family they had so desperately scraped together, inside the slave quarters of a particular plantation. The intensity of black desiring may be measured when one remembers that legal marriage was forbidden for slaves. Yet the records are bursting with accounts demonstrating human feality—as when the freedman saved his earnings over seven or eight years in order to purchase the freedom of his "wife."

Prospering white America perverted, and perverts, the fundamental solace and nurture of community even to the point of derogating the extended family discoverable among America's white and black impoverished; as any college graduate can tell you, the extended family is "compensation for failure." According to these norms, success happens when the man and his immediate family may competently provide for greater and greater privacy, i.e., greater and greater isolation from others, independence from others, capability to delimit and egotistically control the compass of social experience. Faced with the humanly universal dilemma of individual limit, prospering white America has turned away from the normal plunging into expanded family and commitment. Instead, the pursuit of exclusive power—the power to exclude and to manipulate—plus the pursuit of insulating layers of material shell, have preempted the pursuit of community and ridiculed happiness as an invalid, asinine goal.

Blocked by white America, in its questing for community, as the appropriate arena for the appearance and shaping of person, Black America has likewise been blocked, in its wayward efforts to emulate the inhumanity of white compensation. Thus, the traditional routes of suicide, violence and exemplary moral courage have emerged. They have emerged despite the spectacular absence of literature and history to document and support black life. Or perhaps, precisely because the usual tools a people employ in the determining of identity were strictly prohibited, these alternative, bizarre, and heroic methods devolved.

But community does not form by marriage between martyr and a movie star. The hero is one, and we remain the many. We have begun like objects belonging to the blind. We have spent our generations in a scream that wasted in the golden ear. Giant, demon, clown, angel, bastard, bitch, and, nevertheless, a family longing, we have made it to the gates: our hearts hungry on the rocks around the countryside, our hopes the same: our hopes, unsatisfied. Now we have the choice, and we must make that choice our own. We are at the gates.

Who are we?

There has been no choosing until now. Until the university, there is no choice. Education is compulsory. Education has paralleled the history of our black lives; it has been characterized by the punishment of nonconformity, abridgement, withered enthusiasm, distortion, and self-denying censorship. Education has paralleled the life of prospering white America; it has been characterized by reverence for efficiency, cultivation of competence unattended by concern for aim, big white lies, and the mainly successful blackout of black life.

Black students arrive at the university from somewhere. Where is that, exactly? Where is Black America, all of it, from the beginning? Why do we ask? How does it happen that we do not know?

What is the university until we arrive? Is it where the teachers of children receive their training? It is where the powerful become more powerful. It is where the norms of this abnormal power, this America, receive the ultimate worship of propagation. It is where the people become usable parts of the whole machine. Machine is not community.

Is the university where the person learns how to become a valuable member of society? Even so, it is not, the university is not, where the person learns how he is always a valuable member of an always valuable society of people. (It probably takes a college graduate to explain the "higher learning" that does not teach the unearned sanctity and value of each person.)

Yet it waits there, at the end of coercion, the citadel of technique and terminology. At the gates, a temporary freedom plays between the student and the school. Choice confronts both sides. It seems. But like the others who have been violated, whose joy has been bled and viciously assaulted even unto birth, the black student can choose to refuse the university only at incredible cost. He needs power if he will spring free from dependency upon those who exploit, isolate, and finally destroy. If he will liberate "homebase" he must, for a time, separate himself from the identity of the powerless. No. He must learn to assume the identity of the powerless, in a powerful way. No. He must understand homebase. But where is that? Who is he, this student the university chooses to accept? Does the university have any idea?

Fortified by the freaks, the heroes, the saints, the rebels in exile, black students reject the necessity of miracle, where identity is concerned. Every saint and every rebel of Black America reinforces the determination of the majority to achieve a normal, ordinary access to person. The majority knows it is, by definition, incapable of the miraculous. And yet it admires the consequences of black miracle in white America: All of us hunt identity.

And so, the black student enters the gates. Choice of entry is delusional. He must go inside, or perish through dependency. But he rejects the university as it panders to his potential for neither/nor anonymity, or for dysfunctional amnesia. He enters the university and, snatching at the shred reality of freedom-at-last, or first choice, he chooses his family.

The black student clutches at family precisely at that mo-

ment when he enters the ultimate glorification of a society that has rejected him. Why is anyone amazed?

Before this moment, family has been merely given, or else taken away. Finally freed from the obedience, the slavery of childhood, black students choose a family for the first time: "When I was a child, I spoke like a child, I thought like a child, I reasoned like a child; when I became a man, I gave up childish ways. For now we see in a mirror dimly, but then face to face. Now I know in part; then I shall understand fully, even as I have been fully understood."

From our knees, we have fought tall enough to look into the question of the mirror. More than any other people, we cannot afford to forget the mirror is a questioning. And *face to face* we eat together in the dining rooms, we dorm together, sleep together, talk together, love ourselves, together, face to face; the family mirror clears to person in that chosen clarity. We, Black America, on the prospering white American university campus, we come together as students, black students. How shall we humanly compose the knowledge that troubles the mind into ideas of life? How can we be who we are?

Black studies. The engineer, the chemist, the teacher, the lawyer, the architect, if he is black, cannot honorably engage in a career except as black engineer, black architect. *Of course, he must master the competence:* the perspectives of physics, chemistry, economics, and so forth. But he cannot honorably, or realistically, forsake the origins of his possible person. Or she cannot. Nor can he escape the tyranny of ignorance except as he displaces ignorance with study: study of the impersonal, the amorality of the sciences *anchored by black studies.* The urgency of his heart, his breath, demands the knowing of the truth about himself: the truth of black experience. And so, black students, looking for the truth, demand teachers least likely to lie, least likely to perpetuate the traditions of lying—lies that deface the father from the memory of the child. We request black teachers of black studies.

It is not that we believe only black people can understand the black experience. It is rather that we acknowledge the difference between criticism and reality as the difference between the Host and the Parasite.

As Fanon has written, the colonized man does not say he knows the truth, he *is* the truth. Likewise, we do not say we know the truth: we are the truth; we are the living black experience and, therefore, We are the primary sources of information.

For us, there is nothing optional about "black experience" and/or "black studies": we must know ourselves. But theories and assertions do not satisfy anymore. Studies are called for. And, regardless how or where these studies lead, the current facts support every effort to create study alliances among nonwhite or nonprospering white Americans who, all of us, endure as victims of materialism versus our lives.

We look for community. We have already suffered the alternatives to community, to human commitment. We have borne the whiplash of "white studies" unmitigated by the stranger ingredient of humane dedication. Therefore, we cannot, in sanity, pass by the potentiality of black studies: studies of the person consecrated to the preservation of that person.

On the contrary, "white studies" should do likewise: At this date when humankind enjoys wild facility to annihilate, no human study can sanely ignore the emergency requirements for efficient, yes, competent affirmation of the values of life, and that most precious burden of identity that depends, beggarly, on love.

The university may choose among a thousand different responses to black demands, but if the decision bespeaks the traditional process of majority overrule, white choice will sputter to no effect. Like the rest of America that is no longer willing to endure hostile control, Black America will not accept any choice affecting their lives unless they control even the terms under consideration. And if it is true that black rejection of majority overrule will lead to a white-predicted "bloodbath," it is also true that he who makes such a prophecy will bear responsibility for its fulfillment.

Poverty is a bloodbath. Exploitation of human life for material gain is unforgivable-letting-bloodflow for the sake of other currencies. Perforce, the natural element of black children has been the American bloodbath. We know American violence, power, and success. Is the university prepared to teach us something new?

Black studies. White studies: revised. What is the curriculum, what are the standards that only human life threatens to defile and "lower?" Is the curriculum kin to that monstrous metaphor of justice seated, under blindfold, in an attitude and substance of absolute stone? Life appealing to live, and to be, and to know a community that will protect the living simply because we are alive: this is the menace to university curriculum and standards. This is the possibility of survival we must all embrace: the possibility of life, as has been said, by whatever means necessary.

In New York City, the metaphor of Harlem contains the symbol, and the fact, of City College. On that campus, the most recent miracle of Black America has become a manifest reality. There, black and Puerto Rican students have joined to issue what they describe as "the fourth demand." This demand exceeds the scope of lately typical negotiation between school and student. It speaks to community. It reads: "The racial composition of the entering class to reflect the Black and Puerto Rican Population of the New York City Schools."

Obviously, the fourth demand reaches outside the university province and into high school habits of student tragedy. In the predominantly black and Puerto Rican high school nearest City College, the academic diploma rate steadies at 1.2 percent. Since black and Puerto Rican students constitute the majority of public students, and since the majority of them receive no academic diploma, how can the City College reflect their majority status? Either the high schools or the college will have to change almost beyond current planning imagination. To meet the fourth demand, New York City lower schools will have to decide that a 65 per cent dropout rate for students, of any color, is intolerable, and that a 1.2 per cent academic diploma rate, at any high school, cannot continue.

In fact, how will City College continue unless it may admit the children of the city? Will the City College of New York resort to importation of students from Iowa and Maine? The children of the city are black and Puerto Rican; they are the children of suffering and impotence; they are the children coerced into lower grade education that alienates upward of 65 per cent of them so that the majority of this majority disappears into varieties of ruin.

If the university will not teach, will not instruct the lower schools by its example, how will they learn? If the university is not the ultimate teaching institution, the ultimate, the most powerful institution to decree the hope of education, *per se,* what is it?

And yet, City College cries "curriculum" and worries about "standards" even while the future of its conceivable justification, the students of the city schools, disappear except for self-destructive trace.

Black and Puerto Rican students at City College, nevertheless, insist upon the fourth demand; they insist upon community. Serving the positive implications of black studies (*life* studies), students everywhere must insist on new college admission policies that will guide and accelerate necessary, radical change, at all levels of education. Universities must admit the inequities of the civilization they boast. These inequities mean that the children of Other America have been vanquished by the consequences of compulsory, hostile instruction and inescapable, destructive experience.

It is appropriate that the university should literally adopt these living consequences as its own humane privilege, for service. Such embrace waits upon the demonstration of majority conscience. Black America waits upon the demonstration of a conscience that will seek justice with utmost, even ruthless, efficiency.

Yet we do not only wait. Black America moves, headstrong, down toward Damascus. Everybody on the ladder, hanging on identity opposed to the hatred of life. And if we do not name the gods according to the worship of our lives, then what will we worship, in deed?

Erased, Debased, and Encased: The Dynamics of African Educational Colonization in America

BY MICHELE RUSSELL

Michele Russell is a graduate student at Brown University specializing in black liberation and socialist revolutions. In this essay, originally read at the New University conference workshop on Black Studies in December 1969, Russell argues that the relationship of blacks to America has been that of colonials. One of the most insidious forms of this colonialism was the educational system which tried to make blacks abandon their heritage and become mirror images of whites. Black Studies, controlled and manipulated by whites, she maintains, is simply the newest form of colonialism. The only education which is relevant is that which teaches blacks to change their colonial status, gives them lessons in self-defense, and provides the tools to serve the black community.

There was glue and we pasted
colored paper on colored paper,
and on blocks with numbers like 3-4-5
on one side and letters like A-B-C on
the other,
we pasted.
and the glue was like peppermint jelly
   and had an odor that made you want
to lick it.
and we did.
and the whole school was glued to-

Reprinted by permission from *College English* 31, no. 7 (April, 1970): 671–81.

gether for the one purpose of smelling
  bad.
and it did.
but, we had to paste orange on blue
  on purple on green on burnt-sienna
  called brown on philalocyanine
  black, and with a crayon made
  circles,
put dots in them and called them eyes,
put lines on them and called it hair,
and then mouths.
then said,
look teacher,
    oh how lovely, she said.
look mommie,
    oh darling show daddy, she said.
look daddie,
    GREAT, daddie said.
      boy, they were lying bastards.
and we glued.
and it caked on our fingers,
and at recess we wiped it all over
everything,
even ourselves.
but this lumpy substance was our
  education:
and it cracked, flaked and fell apart
  when it dried,
for it too, was white.

                              Carl H. Greene[1]

The schools supplied the servants of the administration. The
products of the schools rose to be clerks, census and tax
counters, interpreters, and chiefs. The teaching in the classroom stressed memory rather than reasoning, repetition by

[1] Published in *Black Expressions,* 1 (Fall 1969).

rote instead of thinking and originality, for these were the ideal moulds for docile civil servants. The purpose of education was not to train for independence, but for subservience.

Oginga Odinga, *Not Yet Uhuru*

Historically, the development of schools and programs for the education of Negroes has represented largely the influences of social forces outside the Negro community and over which he has had little or no control.

Virgil A. Clift, "Educating the American Negro"

One of the most important elements in the current crisis in American higher education is the presence there of large numbers of Blacks: the one national group explicitly committed to insurgency for survival. We are there as students, as faculty members, as omnicompetent administrators and supermasculine menials. In every one of these instances we are exploited, isolated, alienated from ourselves and our communities.

Third World Caucus Statement— NUC National Convention, June 1969

I

Black Skins, White Tasks

THE FUNDAMENTAL RELATIONSHIP of the American nation to the Africans she rules domestically is a colonial one. Originally economically profitable for the colonizer, the changes that advanced industrial development have wrought in the economy have made the black colony in the U.S. peripheral, even expendable, as a labor pool. Our primary use as a group is to keep white lower and middle class people in line by threatening their job security and social hegemony. We can only fulfill this function if we are kept poor enough as a group to be a constant irritant on the society, but docile enough through receipt of public welfare "benefits" and the examples of black "individuals" who have made it so that we don't rise up in massive armed rebellion on the one hand, or leave the country on the other.[2]

Obviously, the line the American nation is treading with regard to us is delicate and is getting shakier all the time. And to those responsible for the economic, political, and social regulation of the American nation (like large corporations, the mass media, the military, the President and all other public officials) the central problem becomes how to control and contain this disruptive element which is *in* but not *of* the nation. Overt slavery isn't popular any more, aside from being difficult to effect when between 35 and 40 million people are involved. But the colonization of the mind is a different matter.

Other New University Conference (NUC) papers have documented how American education shapes the minds and aspirations of white people, and what an efficient channelling instrument it has become where they are concerned.[3] The ways in which that system has moved against blacks is even uglier and more insidious. First of all, it teaches blacks to think they are white. As a position paper from the Center for Black Education in Washington, D.C., correctly states:

One of the results of the rape and penetration of the African continent by the Europeans has been the growth of the assump-

[2] For a collection of analytic perspectives on this situation, see "Colonialism and Liberation in America," special summer 1968 issue of *Viet Report,* and *The Dialectics of Black Power* by Robert Allen (a Guardian pamphlet).

[3] See "The Laying On of Culture" by John McDermott, "The English Teacher as Civilizer" by Barbara Kessel, and "The Community College" by L. & F. Friedman, B. Kessel, R. Rothstein, and R. Wallace. All are publications of the New University Conference.

tion that the only valid and legitimate standards of well-being are those of white supremacy, white power, and white nationalism. White consciousness is always equated as human consciousness. Education is the primary instrument used to instill consciousness. The educational process that we are forced to undergo demands a commitment to white standards and values. It insists that we become white of mind if not white of skin, and that our commitment be to the assumptions, practices, priorities of white supremacy and white nationalism. This assumption is usually phrased as "the struggle for equality." Other examples include "equal" employment, "equal" housing, "equal" pay, "equal" toilets, etc. This, of course, avoids the question of equal to what. This catechism of "equality" only addresses itself to the ever-changing specific manifestations of our oppression.

The current rash of Black Studies Programs, although an apparent departure from the "equal rights" mode of struggle, is only the latest phase in America's domination over us. To understand how serious the situation is, all we need do is compare the major characteristics of African slavery and colonization in the U.S. with the process by which blacks are brought into established institutions of higher education. The parallels are striking and instructive.

In the initial stages of African colonization four things occurred which we can identify as "Before Arrival" (B.A.) prerequisites. First, "recruitment" channels had to be established between European slavers and Africans in positions of trust and power who would act as mercenaries against their people. Secondly, African mercenaries and European colonizers had to cooperate in collecting and selecting large populations "suitable" for transport to the New World. Third, those who were "lucky" enough to be chosen had to undergo the shock of passage, usually with other blacks of different tribes whose local customs had previously set them apart rather than binding them together. And fourth, upon landing in America, the blacks who survived had to submit to a plantation diaspora which was the final complement to the systematic separation and disruption of families and tribes that had begun with recruitment.

Once ensconced in the plantations of the New World, there were still more tests to pass. After a trial period during which Africans were consistently excluded from the language and customs of the plantation social system, it was decided that the slaves could be used most effectively if certain "liberalizing" procedures were followed. To facilitate our ability to take orders (and be satisfied exclusively with that) we were taught only the vocabulary of our specific jobs. To undermine our sense of nationhood and inculcate identification with our masters, there was widespread rape and mongrelization of our people. Once this was accomplished, our colonizers felt it was safe to let us congregate, but only for activities (like religious worship) considered peripheral and non-antagonistic to doing the master's work. And finally, with emancipation (the end of our enforced stay as non-paid workers on the plantation) we were granted the "privilege" of becoming either rural tenant farmers or joining an underemployed urban class and incurring a monetary indebtedness to the system which had been built through our oppression.

With a very slight transposition of vocabulary (for Before Arrival, read Bachelor of Arts; for Africa, read the South and for New World, the North; for diaspora, read brain drain; for plantation, read college system; for mongrelization, read integration and cultural diversity programs; for religious worship, substitute Black Studies; and for tenant farming, substitute the monetary aid system by which black students are consistently given loans over scholarships) the whole process becomes a perfect metaphor of the dynamics of black educational colonization in America.

Even though we've now come to the point of at least rhetorical rebellion against this kind of channelling, a look at the so-called "black" programs which white, racist institutions are letting us have, reveals that colleges are conceding space not out of fear of our power, black power, but from a sense of their own strength. Administrators and faculty members can feel secure precisely because they know that elementary and secondary education is efficient enough so that by age 18, the students who demand Black Studies will themselves devise programs which mirror the tendencies of interinstitutional and interpersonal competition, brain drain and diaspora which American institutions are organized to perpetuate in everyone —white, black, or red—whom they educate. I mean, like, man, if you don't have at least 2½ pints militant rhetoric for every vacant square inch of student body, you're like nowhere, man.

And as if this ethos weren't debilitating enough for a people trying to build communal consciousness, the "authorities" intervene to shape these programs so that: 1) they foster a "showplace" or "laboratory" mentality where black people are reduced to pathologies for white students of "the problem" and our "deviations" from the American mainstream are examined, "all the better to see you, my dear," and 2) some black students are given the illusion of sanctuary and of having infinite time to explore themselves and the world around them, while others are inculcated with a very particular kind of urgency: one which pushes them into acquiring skills and adopting career aspirations which dovetail neatly into a federal funding calendar. In this way we are led from teacher's aid programs, to anti-poverty careers (which depend for their existence on the continuation of poverty), to becoming sociologists, to the latest thing: biological technicians and psychotherapists. The reasoning seems to be if you can't educate someone out of their blackness, you might be able to starve them out. If they won't take starvation, you try to convince them that their hunger is a product of social forces too complex for them to understand and their lives are "problems-to-be-solved." If that doesn't work, and in spite of everything they continue to reproduce, you talk to them about how overpopulated the world is and refuse them their welfare checks if they don't take the pill. And when they not only continue to increase, but begin to talk about systematic genocide, you send in the psychologists to declare universal black paranoia and cart us off to mental institutions where "rehabilitation" consists of redefining our sense of oppression in *personal, inner-directed* terms. Always hiding the face of the enemy.

Because of America's sophisticated educational system, these maneuvers needn't even be performed by white people any more. We've got our own native colonizers: a whole class of black people trained not even in terms of filling national manpower needs, but in order to contain the black population, to isolate us as much as possible, to institutionalize our colonial status as both expendable and marginal. To effect one kind of black control of the black community.

II

From "Didn't My Lord Deliver Daniel"
to "Steal Away to Freedom"

The cultural consequences and ramifications of this domination have been extensive. Until 1865 it was a crime punishable by death for black people to learn how to read and write. In the isolated instances where white individuals or organizations like the American Missionary Association took it upon themselves to educate Africans, it was always in a religious context and for the purpose of stressing the possibility of posthumous salvation. As the institution of slavery could be perversely rationalized as the extension of the gospel of hard work, so "Christianizing" the "heathens" became the accepted substitute for freeing the slaves: salving white consciences by saving black souls.

Through the resiliency of African culture, however (as much as through the unrelenting nature of Euro-American oppression) the Judeo-Christian scripture of dreams deferred were transformed into potent incantations of black revenge. Nat Turner took the mission of the avenging prophet to heart. Africans who had been taught to sing "Didn't My Lord Deliver Daniel" began to "Follow the Drinking Gourd" in earnest and to "Steal Away to Freedom" cause they were "So Tired a Dis Mess." As a means of physical containment, this first step in America's educational subjugation of Africans met with little success. It was very effective in establishing the black church as the primary *institutional* channel through which our anger, pain, and aspirations were mediated,[4] but it couldn't undercut the black masses' struggle for secular freedom that peaked during the mid-nineteenth century.

As the African population in America became more and more unmanageable, as insurrections multiplied and fugitives increased, the American government decided it was in the interests of national stability to temper its original position.[5] Despite the popularity of the colonization movements of the

[4] See E. Franklin Frazier, *The Negro Church in America* (Schocken, 1964), and Albert Cleage, *The Black Messiah* (Sheed & Ward, 1969).
[5] See John Hope Franklin, *From Slavery to Freedom* (Alfred A. Knopf, 1966).

early nineteenth century among whites,[6] the growing sectional divisions in the country made it more dangerous for blacks to think of themselves as uprooted Africans than as American Negroes. A civil war had to be fought, and black men in uniform were crucial to Union victory.

Hence, Emancipation, and the next hundred years (i.e., until 1965). We black people had been so-called "freed" to recast ourselves in the mold of full-fledged Americans rather than to continue to conduct ourselves as an oppressed alien population. But in order to insure that we kept our hands on the plow while our eyes were on the prize (trans: continued to work for the master while we concentrated on how to get his foot off our necks) we had to be educated to believe that *the*

[6] One expression of the missionary impulse just mentioned was the establishment of organizations like the American Colonization Society (1812), which exerted pressure upon freedmen to leave the country for settlement in Africa. The supporters of the colonization movement espoused the theory of "Providential design," viz., that God has allowed a portion of the African population to be enslaved and brought to America where it had been "Christianized" and "civilized" for the purpose of cultivating a group among them who would "return" and "redeem" Africa, not to mention keeping it open for continued European economic penetration (for contemporary counterpart, substitute Peace Corps). It was hoped that this strategy would serve as a safety valve, ridding America of the most militant blacks and redirecting their energies so as to prevent them from organizing their fellow slaves in the "new world" around "life, liberty, and the pursuit of happiness" before death. Abraham Lincoln himself was a strong supporter of this approach to solving the nation's racial contradictions and in August of 1862 he called a group of prominent free Negroes to the White House to urge them to support colonization saying: "Your race suffer greatly, many of them, by living among us, while ours suffer from your presence. In a word, we suffer on each side. If this is admitted, it affords a reason why we should be separated." As John Hope Franklin points out (p. 281): "Largely at Lincoln's suggestion, the State Department made inquiries of South American governments and of some insular and African governments concerning the possibility of colonizing American Negroes. . . . Down to the end of the war Lincoln held out hope for colonizing at least some of the Negroes who were being set free."

agent of oppression was also the source of liberation. The foot on our necks was being moved to a rearguard position and we were told that we should crave the kick in the ass from plantation to ghetto that the master's boot provided. In educational terms, that was called "becoming well-rounded." And the primary vehicle for acculturation was the Negro college, funded by white philanthropy.[7]

Since 1965, with the experiences of civil rights struggles behind us and the thoughts of Malcolm X and fellow fighters in the Third World made available to us (posthumously and in cut-rate editions, courtesy of Grove Press), the absurdity of our publicly held posture in this country—head bowed, pants down, skirts up, hands clasped in prayer, waiting to be violated—has become clear. And we see the need to re-cover ourselves: both in the sense of "getting ourselves together" and of doing it quietly, among ourselves. The reasons for this decision are historical as well as tactical.

There has always been a great discrepancy between how we black people have appeared to whites, our institutional oppressors, and how we have shown ourselves to one another. This has been a necessary part of our survival: individually and collectively. As Henry Bibb remarked in the narrative of his existence as a slave, "The only weapon of self-defense I could use successfully was that of deception." So when we talk about our "public posture" we are talking about a very self-conscious manner arrived at by asking the questions: What portion of ourselves, our lives, can we put up for sale? What

[7] Between the end of the Civil War and the beginning of World War I, the following large educational foundations were begun specifically to advance southern Negro education: the Peabody Education Fund, the John F. Slater Fund, the General Education Board (a Rockefeller subsidiary), the Anna T. Jeanes Fund, the Julius Rosenwald Fund, and the Phelps-Stokes Fund.

expendables can we exchange with Chuck for some time, air, and breathing space? And crucially, what can we show him of ourselves that will convince him that our use of time, air, and space won't be a threat to his existence? Booker T. Washington had one response to these questions, W. E. B. Du Bois had another, the mass of black people had a third. All three posed problems.

Washington was convinced that whites in America would never believe that Africans were the equals of Europeans. He also knew that the cultural arrogance of Euro-Americans led them into adopting a hierarchy of human attributes (despite the Jeffersonian model of the "noble husbandman") which placed proficiency in technical skills at a lower level of importance than so-called "intellectual alacrity" and even went so far in some cases as to divorce one ability from the other. Playing on this bias and knowing that the group survival of blacks rested on our becoming efficient producers in self-reliant communities, he publicly conceded the argument over black inferiority and concentrated on developing a system of black aspirations which was complementary to white prejudice, American industrial development, and consistent with his own view of group progress. He said: "For years to come the education of the people of my race should be so directed that the greatest proportion of the mental strength of the masses will be brought to bear upon the everyday practical things of life, upon something that is needed to be done, *and something which they will be permitted to do* in the community in which they reside" [my emphasis]. Unfortunately, this strategy left Washington completely at the mercy of white philanthropy for funds, the whims of southern whites for implementation, and the national focus of the program led to a system of educational priorities decided in terms of America's needs rather than those of black people.

Du Bois, Harvard educated and for a large part of his life European-oriented, fought unflaggingly against Washington's position. In *Souls of Black Folk,* he makes these specific criticisms:

1. He is striving nobly to make Negro artisans businessmen and property-owners; but it is utterly impossible, under modern competitive methods, for workingmen and property-owners to defend their rights and exist without the right of suffrage.
2. He insists on thrift and self-respect, but at the same time counsels a silent submission to civic inferiority such as is bound to sap the manhood of any race in the long run.
3. He advocates common-school and industrial training, and depreciates institutions of higher learning; but neither the Negro common-schools, nor Tuskegee itself, could remain open a day were it not for teachers trained in Negro colleges, or trained by their graduates (p. 49).

"Absolutely certain that the way for a people to gain respect is not by continually belittling and ridiculing themselves," Du Bois urged "the thinking classes of American Negroes" "to state plainly and unequivocally the legitimate demands of their people" (p. 51). The truth, says Du Bois, shall make us free. The danger in this rationalist view of the world is that it leads the great black theorist into such a veneration for knowledge that his vision of black nirvana at the time of this controversy is a "classical" education at the end of which: "I sit with Shakespeare and he winces not. Across the color line I move arm in arm with Balzac and Dumas, where smiling men and welcoming women glide in gilded halls. From out the caves of evening that swing between the strong-limbed earth and the tracery of stars, I summon Aristotle and Aurelius and what soul I will, and they come all graciously with no scorn nor condescension. So, wed with Truth, I dwell above the Veil" (p. 87).

The contemporary articulation of this hope is that Harvard institute open admissions so that everyone will be allowed to participate in white ruling class culture. In Du Bois's resolution, the part of ourselves we show white Americans to convince them that our use of time, air, and space won't be a threat is that part which strives to be like them at their best. Very flattering to the rulers. But what about the masses of black people who have neither leisure, nor reasonableness, nor shared ruling class tastes with which to bargain? How can we survive publicly?

Historically, the people have dealt with the problem by bartering the only resource we possessed in abundance: the collective culture we have forged out of the stuff of our oppression. The group education we had to practice among ourselves almost without thinking was transmitted from generation to generation by word of mouth, by doing dozens, by Shine swimming on. This culture defied Western categories. It arose from the masses of the inarticulate. Its essence disappeared when put on display. It left no artifacts. It was "the whole body of efforts made by a people to describe, justify, and praise the action through which that people had created itself and kept itself in existence." It became rich and abundant because we knew that being adept artificers and surviving were coterminous. Performance was for internal strength and against discovery and always went on in the context of the struggle to keep the integrity of the individual and the group intact. It became the repository of our dreams, the medium where our own version of Reconstruction took shape, enabling us to step to a different drummer in another country. And when just enough of the code attained popular usage (as in black music) so that the gulf between our lives and those of Euro-Americans became apparent, we tried to show our rulers our culture in ways which would interest and amuse them while stopping short of revealing the antagonisms in the discrepancies. As Piri Thomas recalls the wisdom of his Black Southern father in *Down These Mean Streets:* "The Indian fought the white man and died. An' us black folk jus' wagged ouah tails, Yas suhses', smiled and multiplied" (pp. 126–7).

Fortunately for us, one of the greatest weaknesses of modern western thought is in the confusion of *culture* with *entertainment*. And because of the alienating organization of industrial capitalism, Americans assume that *entertainment,* the realm where they can enjoy themselves, is only possible during *leisure* time. And niggers only have leisure time if they steal it or if they're "shiftless-like-we-always-knew-they-were-anyway." Hence, the whole proliferation of stereotypes surrounding Stepinfetchit-Sambos: all a creation of the contortions forced upon Africans by Europeans.

But the stereotypes, too, we blacks thought we could use to our own advantage. We thought that because of their myopia, white Americans had only absorbed the mudsill: the public Negro culture of entertainment a la Ethel Waters, Amos n Andy, and Sammy Davis Jr. which we could embroider at will and package in whatever cosmetics Clairol would pay us to model, whatever sides Motown could sell. As a people, we thought we could still remain intact, reserving for ourselves that deep and rich cultural substratum of struggle, of black life which remains covert, coded, dynamic; of black arts with which we could change reality; of black artists whose juju could conjure black spirits to hurl against the white mountain of hate and sustain us, black people, in the face of it. We even thought we could use poems as guns and that it was a sign of *our* strength that we could get up on national TV and call the man a mothahfuckah to his face with a jazz background and live to see the prime-time replay.

It's only now that we are beginning to see that it's *all* been a prime-time replay. We are beginning to see that there's a reason why Malcolm X is dead and Elijah Muhammad is alive (see Booker T. Washington's solution). There's a reason why Fred Hampton gets murdered in his sleep by Chicago's "defenders of the piece," but Cornell's faculty and administration praise brothers who protect themselves and their sisters on an Ithaca campus with guns (Du Bois's strategy). And a reason why the Rockefeller and Ford Foundations have all but abandoned undergraduate aid to Negro colleges in the south and have instead instituted three new fellowship programs for black graduate students and faculty from the south to go north for post-graduate work (diaspora). And there's even a reason why soon you will be able to get more foundation, corporation, and federal money than you can ask for to set up pilot programs in the public schools for teaching non-standard English, for training black para-professionals in new careers, and setting up all manner of *institutional* experiments in the ghettos[8] (even to the extent of letting LeRoi Jones play poet/ priest/politician in Newark), but you will find it impossible to get funds to pay individual parents to conduct in-the-home education for the extended families they feed, clothe, and shelter (culture-power to the people as long as it's out in the open).

Don't misunderstand me. There's no back-room conspiracy

[8] Like Headstart, the "Higher Horizons Program" in New York City, and the "Great Cities Project" in 14 major cities supported with Ford Foundation funds, all of which "operate on the assumption that present problems of the culturally deprived (read: black) youth in our schools can be solved by an expansion of services that have worked with middle-class white children. These are sometimes referred to as 'saturation programs' which provide for more guidance, more remedial instruction, more emphasis on reading, more individual psychological testing, and more cultural programs." "Educating the American Negro," by Virgil A. Clift, *American Negro Reference Book* (1966).

afoot. There is, however, a parlor strategy. And it's based in part on the realization that Henry Bibb's statement of how his life was preserved by artifice didn't only mean that here was "another sly nigger," but that for him and millions of his brothers and sisters there was (and still is) no division between art and life and that the source of our people's politics (in the root sense of lives in the "polis" or societal unit) has proceeded from that expression which white America had for so long thought was mere entertainment.

Now that the colonizers had become hip, the next step was painfully obvious. All the nation had to do to contain our politics was to contain our culture. And not by stripping us of it, but by publicizing it. Giving courses in it. Institutionalizing its validity. If the subject is art, emphasize African sculpture because it is quintessentially a-historical. If the subject is music, canonize those modes from jazz and blues which have been most successfully (profitably) appropriated and marketed by Europeans. And if the subject is literature, force our oral and written expression into the sterile straitjacket of genre so that it may be considered on a par with European literature. And at every step of the way, stratify our culture, make it static, elevate it to a plane higher than life, abstract it so as to negate all those ingredients of struggle which have until now made it an arena of black decolonization and liberation. Sidetrack us into arguments over whether a black or white face interprets our past for us, but be careful, whichever wins out, to keep the inquiry disinterested and the applications remote.

Our oppressors' inventiveness would increase. Letting us change that first vision of the slave begging to be raped "kindly" instead of brutally to a soulfoodeating afrobearing dashikiwearing guntoting poetryspouting boogalooing fistwaving dude—as long as we kept him in sight. Making us believe in the McLuhan notion of the "age of circuitry" and rely more and more on the oppressor's media to carry our messages for us. Making our *lives,* in this nation which already has the highest standard of living in the world, available for public *consumption*—as *entertainment* for Euro-Americans. Going even further, and perpetrating the final irony: making consumer culture so seductive that we black people join the pack and wind up devouring ourselves. Thus, not only is our culture being institutionalized as entertainment, but black politics, black life, black oppression as well.[9] That is why we are now

[9] Witness the following account of the Chicago Conspiracy Trial in LIFE magazine, November 14, 1969:

"In Chicago the Conspiracy Eight trial was looking and sounding more and more like the Theater of the Absurd. In fact, it had become the hottest show in town, heavily patronized by the Junior League and the Social Register. Beautiful People coaxed passes from lawyer husbands or acquaintances in the press and took their seats in the tiny courtroom. Outside the courtroom, family, friends of the defendants and yippie sympathizers were turned away by marshals because of the 'lack of space.' For other society ladies, going to the trial was too much, so they had the trial come to them. To have one's very own conspirator-in-residence at a party was suddenly the ultimate in cachet. The out-on-bail conspirator gives a little rap, the ladies open their checkbooks, they feel a little less guilty, the conspirator leaves with the loot—all for the cause, of course.

"Onstage the big attraction was one of the leads, Black Panther defendant Bobby Seale. Along with the seven others, he was charged with incitement to riot during the 1968 Democratic Convention. But Seale insisted his constitutional rights were being violated because the judge would not allow him to act as his own defense counsel, and he made absolutely sure that everybody—including the jury and (certainly) the press—knew of his extreme displeasure. As 25 witnesses for the government's prosecution testified, Seale constantly jumped to his feet, peppering Judge Julius J. Hoffman with obscenities and labels that ranged from 'fascist' to 'pig.' Pig is what did it. After repeated warnings, Hoffman ordered Seale shackled to his chair and gagged. At first Seale screamed right through the adhesive tape, and clanked his chains. On the second day he slumped over on a table, looking woozy. Copies of a note written by Seale earlier that morning circulated through the courtroom, saying that marshals had attempted to stuff rags down his

at that point where our recovery requires our re-covery and we see that *no public posture can secure our group survival.* As Aretha would say, there jus' ain' no way.

III

"Let us not be the instrument of our own oppression."
—South African Youth League

This conclusion leaves us with a huge task—the one we've always had, undiminished: black revolution and nationbuilding. And at this stage of the struggle, education for defense is paramount. This front is particularly hard to move on because it requires self-reliance and group trust—those things we have experienced least. It requires creating a whole underground communications network (i.e., educational system) capable of feeding survival information to the masses of our people. It means that we have to disappear from so-called "liberal arts" programs in existing accredited educational institutions, only reappearing for specific technical training consistent with changing our colonial status. It means that the educational process must not be contained within any single physical facility. It means breaking our dependency on whites and becoming producers instead of consumers. We must acquire those skills which will put us in a position as a group to free our minds to serve our people, to provide goods and services to

---

throat, choking him, and that the tape on his head cut off the circulation. After three days of this spectacle, the judge ordered Seale's restraints removed, whereupon a group of respected lawyers, claiming that Hoffman was violating Seale's civil rights, appealed to the federal government to let Seale defend himself. But before that decision could be made, Judge Hoffman suddenly announced a mistrial for Seale and then sentenced him to four years for contempt."

sustain our people, and to control the necessary mechanisms of force and violence to protect our people.

Education for defense requires that we come to terms with our history as an African people, and take up the thread of that history where Europeans forced us to relinquish it 400 years ago. Our thrust must be toward consolidation and not further fragmentation. As Junebug Jabbo Jones has said: "The struggle of African people is for an African nation. While it is important that a number of battles for self-reliance be waged in the Americas by African people, we should always see those battles in relation to the struggle for an independent African continent. We should not content ourselves with living among other races *simply* by their permission of their endurance."

America is the land we must overcome, Africa is the land we must win. Our people must possess the mental and material resources necessary to wage that fight. If we prepare the ground well for defense, it will nourish the seeds of our liberation.

The Case for Black Studies

BY DEVERE E. PENTONY

DeVere E. Pentony, dean of the School of Behavioral and Social Sciences at San Francisco State College, received his Ph.D. from the University of Iowa and is the author of several books on international relations. Pentony agrees with Harding and Jordan that the major focus of Black Studies must be on helping blacks to discover their identity and to prepare leaders for the black community. The concern with blackness is a corrective to white racism and will inevitably, Pentony asserts, lead to some antiwhiteness. If there is any indoctrination by black teachers professing a certain ideology, Pentony argues that this will be no worse than white teachers who do the same thing. If colleges can attract black scholars with a passion for truth and open their programs to all students, Pentony believes that black students will develop a sense of pride and white students will be able to develop new perspectives about black men and women.

THE HISTORY of the development of various American groups into an integrated culture is a complex story, but there is one simple fact that seems germane to the problems of black-white integration in the United States. This obvious fact is that almost every immigrant group with the major exception of the blacks came to these shores because they wanted to come. America was to be the land of opportunity, the land where the rigidities for social mobility would be relaxed, and the land where a man could be free. That these expectations were not quickly fulfilled is a cloudy part of the political and social history of the United States, but in retrospect the members of most of these groups, the Irish, the Germans, the Dutch, the

Reprinted by permission from *The Atlantic Monthly* CCXXII (April, 1969): 81–82, 87–89.

Scotch, the Italians now view the story of their ethnic past in the United States as a reasonably successful one.

No similar memories have been available to the black man and woman. Brought to this country in chains, torn from family and tribal past, physically and psychologically enslaved, taught by lash and example to be subservient, forced to suffer indignities to their basic humanity, and instantly categorized by the accident of color, black people have all too often found the American dream a nightmare. Instead of joining the dominant culture, many have learned to exist in the psychologically bewildering atmosphere neither slave nor free. That they have survived at all is tribute to their magnificent resiliency and basic toughness; but that some carry with them a heavy baggage of hate and rage is not surprising.

While many whites in America have congratulated themselves upon the progress toward freedom and equality that has recently been made, a number of black intellectuals are eloquently questioning whether, indeed, meaningful progress has been made. Perhaps blacks are all too familiar with the ability of white people to dash black hopes for freedom and dignity on rocks of intransigence and patience. Witness the rise and fall of hope in the story of black men in America: in the aftermath of the Civil War they were told that they were freed from slavery only to find that they were not free—not free to be treated as individuals, not free to eat, or sleep, or live, or go to school, or drink from the same fountain, or ride the same conveyance, or enjoy the same political and economic privileges as people of "white" skin. And when in the twentieth century they had their hopes raised by long overdue court decisions and civil rights legislation finally demanding integration, these hopes were once again shattered as blacks found that significant segments of the white culture often lagged far behind the basic justice of these acts.

This has led some of the black community to question whether integration was not just another scheme to preserve the dominance of the whites, seducing blacks to give up their black identities and to copy the speech, manner, hair, dress, and style of the whites, and to accept the myths, heroes, and historical judgment of white America without reciprocity or without appreciation of, or respect for, black experience. Moreover, this estimate has been coupled with the hunch that in any significant way, only the "talented tenth" of the black community could really hope to overcome the monetary, social, and psychological barriers to true integration with whites. The remaining 90 per cent would, therefore, be left in poverty and psychological degradation, doomed to an almost motiveless, hopeless existence, forever on the dole, forever caught in hate of self and of others. Thus has been posed a transcendent dilemma for the black man and woman: to succeed in the white world is to fail, to overcome the outrageous obstacles thrown in their way by white society seems partially to deny their black experience. Above all, to integrate on an individual basis in a society that makes this increasingly possible for the fortunate may well mean an exodus of the talented tenth from the black community, with the consequent decimation of the ranks of potential leaders whose commitment to the whole community could help set their people free.

Seen in this light, the demand for black studies is a call for black leadership. The argument is that if there is to be an exodus from the land of physical and psychological bondage, an informed and dedicated leadership is needed to help bring about individual and group pride and a sense of cohesive community. To accomplish this, black people, like all people, need to know that they are not alone. They need to know that their ancestors were not just slaves laboring under the white man's sun but that their lineage can be traced to important kingdoms and significant civilizations. They need to be familiar with the black man's contribution to the arts and sciences. They need to know of black heroes and of the noble deeds of black men. They need to know that black, too, is beautiful, and that under the African sky people are at proud ease with their blackness. In historical perspective they need to know the whole story of white oppression and of the struggles of some blacks, and some whites too, to overcome that oppression. They need to find sympathetic encouragement to move successfully into the socioeconomic arenas of American life.

To help fulfill all these needs, the contention is, a black studies effort must be launched. At the beginning, it must be staffed by black faculty, who must have the time and resources to prepare a solid curriculum for college students and to get the new knowledge and new perspectives into the community as quickly as possible. In a situation somewhat similar to the tremendous efforts at adult education in some of the less developed societies, the advocates of black studies press to get on with the urgent tasks.

It is in this context that a basic challenge is made to many of the traditional values of the college or university. Important critical questions arise: Will black studies be merely an exchange of old lies for new myths? Is it the work of the college to provide an ideological underpinning for social movement? Will the traditional search for the truth be subordinated to the goal of building a particular group identity? Is the ideal of the brotherhood of all men to be sacrificed to the brotherhood of some men and the hatred of others? Can the college teach group solidarity for some groups and not for others? Will the results of separatist studies be a heightening of group tensions and a reactive enlarging of the forces of racism? Will standards of excellence for students and faculty alike be cast aside in the interest of meeting student and community needs? Will anti-intellectualism run rampant? Will constitutional and other legal provisions be violated by this new version of "separate if not equal"?

A Remedy for White Studies

It seems clear that the advocates of a black studies program see it as a remedy for "white studies" programs that they have been subjected to all their lives and as a way to bring pride, dignity, and community to black people. They are questioning the relevance of the style and content of education designed to meet the needs and expectations of the dominant white culture, and some seem to be suggesting that the life-styles and ways of perceiving the world in much of the black community are sufficiently different to justify a new, almost bicultural approach to educating the members of the community who are at once a part of, yet apart from, the general American culture. While they hope that this effort will range over the whole educational experience from childhood through adulthood, they seem to view the college or university as the place where talents can be gathered and resources mobilized to provide intellectual leadership and academic respectability to their efforts. The college is to be the place for the writing of books, the providing of information, and the training of students to help with the critical tasks. It is to be one of the testing grounds for the idea that black people need to have control of their own destiny.

But what of the outcome? There is obvious concern that efforts to focus on blackness as one of the answers to white racism will result in an equally virulent black racism. Black "nationalism," with its glorifying of the black ingroup, may have powerful meaning only when it focuses on the hate object of whiteness. Indeed, it is painfully true that whites through their words and deeds over many generations have provided the black nationalists with all the bitter evidence they need for building a negative nationalism based mainly on hatred and rage. Thus we should expect that a significant ingredient in constructing black unity and group dignity would be an anti-whiteness.

Increasingly, the black intellectual is drawing a colonial analogy to the situation of the black community in the United States. Like people in the colonized lands of Asia, Africa, and Latin America, some black men look at their rather systematic exclusion from first-class citizenship in the United States as a close parallel to the exploitation and subjugation perpetrated by those who shouldered the "white man's burden" during the high tide of imperialism. Thus the focus on black culture and black history is to prepare the black community to be as free and proud as anyone in the newly emerging states. And the outcome of that may be the growth of the self-confidence and sense of personal dignity that pave the way for an easier integration into a common culture on the basis of feelings of real equality.

While it would be foolish to deny that ugly and self-defeating racism may be the fruits of the black studies movement, we should not forget that a sense of deep compassion and intense concern for all humanity has often shone through the rage and hate of such prophets of the movement as Malcolm X, Stokely Carmichael, and W. E. B. Du Bois. Whether that hopeful strain of compassion and human concern will gain the upper hand in the days that lie ahead may well depend on the degree of understanding and tenderness with which the white community is able to react to these efforts.

There is the possibility that an emphasis on blackness, black dignity, black contributions, and black history will provide whites with new perspectives about the black man and woman. In turn, these new perspectives may indicate what clues of behavior and guides to proper responsiveness are necessary to enable whites to relate to blacks in something other than a patronizing or deprecating fashion. Through black studies there may be opportunities for whites to enrich their understanding of the black man and thus, perhaps, to help build more meaningful bridges of mutual respect and obligation. Moreover, if the truth can make blacks free and open, it may also free the whites from their ignorant stereotypes of the black man and his culture. Unfortunately, it may also be possible for those who teach black studies to reinforce those stereotypes by aping the worst features of the white society and becoming merely a mirror image of that aspect of white society that is insensitive and inhuman.

Standards and Scholarship

Will accepted standards and scholarship be maintained in the black studies program? When any new program is proposed, a question of this sort is certainly appropriate for members of the academic community. However, it is an extremely difficult one to answer for a black studies program or for any other new program. All that can be safely said is that the pressures for respectable scholarly performance and for recognized achievements will be at least as great for black studies as for any other new program.

In the performance and evaluation of students, we can probably expect the same ferment over learning, grading, and evaluating practices that perturbs the rest of the academic world. But academicians who are pushing the black studies idea give no indication that they will be content with a half-hearted, sloppy, shoddy intellectual effort on the part of themselves or their students. Indeed, one of the underlying assumptions of black studies seems to be that students who become involved in it will become highly motivated toward academic success not only in black studies but in the rest of the curriculum as well. Out of the black studies experience are to come black students, committed, socially aware, ambitious, devoted to the welfare of black people, and equipped for helping the black community assume its rightful place in American society. These are high ambitions which are not likely to be fulfilled immediately by a black studies program, but which deserve to be given the same benefit of doubt and the same opportunities for growth by trial and error that most new programs are given.

Will black studies scholars manipulate data, bias their studies, and create towering myths which bear little resemblance to the shifting realities of human existence? The answer is difficult to assess.

In one respect the quest for pristine outside objectivity may miss the point. A distinguished philosopher has argued that the search for intergroup accommodation must be based upon what he terms the discovery of the normative inner order—that is, the values, assumptions, and world views or images of various societies or cultures. It may be that one of the most important roles that the black scholar can play is to share in the discovery and articulation of this normative inner order of the black community, with the possible result of improving the chances for mutually beneficial black-white interaction.

In this process we should expect that there will be black professors who profess a certain "ideology" just as white professors do. We can even expect a case for racial superiority of blacks, but surely this is not a reason for opposing black studies. To do so on those grounds would be analogous to opposing the teaching of biology because a certain biologist has attempted to make a case for a black inferiority based on some of his genetic investigations, or of economics because certain economists continue to adhere to pre-Keynesian economic principles.

Moreover, the ideology argument may mean no more than that black scholars will attempt to emphasize common assumptions about American society from the perspective of the black experience. But this kind of "indoctrination" is not essentially different from what is found, for example, in many college textbooks in American government which rest on some value-laden assumptions about the American political system. A more serious charge would be that black professors may insist that their students follow some "party line" as they examine the various facets of the black situation. But students are not as gullible as we sometimes imagine and are generally quite capable of resisting efforts at indoctrination.

Closely allied to the questions of standards and scholarship are questions of curriculum. What is an appropriate beginning curriculum for a black studies effort? The unspoken consensus seems to be that an area studies program should dig as deeply as possible into the history, the culture, the language, the politics, the economics, the geography, the literature, the arts, the life-styles, and the world views of the people in the area concerned. How this is all put together in a way that students will understand and benefit from is a significant organizing problem for all area studies programs, including black studies. But it would be foolish to expect those problems to be creatively attacked before a working faculty is on the scene. The first efforts to establish a satisfactory curriculum in black studies will be experimental in many ways and as such subject to more rapid change than our established curricula.

Are Black Studies Legal and Proper?

The question of legality of a black studies program requires examination. Like the closely related area studies program, the curriculum would seem to face no legal questions from federal or state law. However, it is in the realm of staffing and student access that the most serious questions arise. For example, can tests of color be applied for hiring faculty members in the black studies program? Posed in this sharp way, the answer to the question is probably no. The equal protection of the laws section of the United States Constitution and various state legal requirements about nondiscrimination in employment could very likely be interpreted to preclude the hiring of faculty simply because they are black. However, if the qualifications for hiring are put on a broader experiential basis than color alone, then the questions and answers may change. Already factors of ethnic background and experience play a role in hiring at the colleges and universities in the United States. While this is particularly obvious in the hiring of teachers in foreign languages and literature—note, for example, the number of people teaching Chinese language and literature who are Chinese—ethnic background has often been considered in other aspects of area studies and other programs from the Peace Corps to social work.

The question of hiring black faculty is probably not a legal question at all. Rather the critical focal point for the black studies program would seem to be, on the one hand, whether the particular experiences gained from a black ethnic background tend to make the faculty member a better scholar and teacher or, on the other hand, whether the ethnic emotional involvement will permit a useful scholarly detachment in the evaluation and presentation of data. Completely satisfactory answers to this dilemma are not likely to be found. A short-run solution to the dilemma may rest on the ability of black studies programs to attract black faculty with a passion for the truth as well as an emotional identification with the subject of blackness, and on the certainty that nonblack scholars will continue to view, comment upon, and analyze the black experience in various parts of the academic community. Enough flexibility and openness should exist for students majoring in black studies to encounter the views of nonblack scholars. Similarly, the educational experiences of the rest of the academic community would undoubtedly be enriched by the participation of black studies faculty in the general intellectual life of the college. It would be tragic if the black studies faculty were to be prevented from commentary on the general questions of man in society by their own preoccupation with black studies. Few would argue that the infusion of an increasing number of black faculty into the academic community is not desirable. The black studies program would speed the process and provide the black community with incentives and opportunities for greater participation in the education of youth. The institutions of higher education cannot rely on narrow legal interpretation and conventional dogmas as trustworthy guidelines to hiring faculty in programs like black studies.

A second serious question about the legality of the black studies program is the question of student access to it. Can an academic institution worthy of the name deny access to any of its academic programs on the basis of color or ethnic background? The answer is no. Here the legal answer and the moral answer would seem to reinforce one another. If one of the purposes of the black studies program is to tell it as it really is, then the message should go out to students regardless of color even though it is likely to have a particular additional value to the black student. The college cannot be a place where knowledge is developed and subjects taught in semi-secret. Just as any college contracting to the government for secret research would be open to serious charge of violation of the traditional ethics of scholarship, so would any academic program that excluded students solely on the basis of ethnic background raise serious questions of propriety and legality.

However, even in this connection a dilemma remains. As anyone who has participated in an area program in a Peace Corps training effort knows, the things that can be easily said about one's own culture and about another culture tend to be modified when there are members of another culture in attendance. It seems to become more difficult to tell it "as it really is" or at least as it "really is perceived" when the outsiders are in. This is a significant problem that will have to be faced by the black studies program. The fortunate thing about many of those who are advocating black studies is that they want to tell it as it really is to anyone who will listen. They have been shielding their feelings, perceptions, and analyses so long that it will probably be refreshing for them to speak honestly with nonblack students as well as blacks. Nonetheless, they may feel that the first efforts to get their programs established will be so overrun by well-meaning whites anxious to gain new perspectives that black students will not have access to the courses.

In practice, the problem may not be so great, especially since courses about various ethnic communities will continue to be offered in the existing departments, with even the possibility of exchange of faculty on occasion. Nonetheless, the colleges must make every effort within the budgetary limitations imposed upon them to accommodate as many students as possible. No black student who enters the college should be denied an opportunity to take black studies courses; neither, of course, should he be forced to do so. In this connection, the attractiveness of the course offerings to whites as well as blacks may be important in the effort to sustain enrollments in a fledgling program, and thus help provide the necessary resources which are closely tied to the level of student demand for courses. So, the question of student access seems to be not so much a question of legality as of the availability of faculty and other resources.

A sometime country lawyer once said: "The dogmas of the quiet past are inadequate to the stormy present. The occasion is piled high with difficulty, and we must rise to the occasion. As our case is new, so we must think anew and act anew. We must disenthrall ourselves, and then we shall save the country" (Abraham Lincoln). The time is now for higher education to show that it can disenthrall itself and become relevant to the problems of social change highlighted by the call for black studies. If a black studies program serves only to awaken whites to the desperate need to change themselves, it will have been worth the effort.

PART TWO

Questions

Race and Reform

BY ELDON L. JOHNSON

Eldon L. Johnson received his Ph.D. from the London School of Economics and Political Science. He has been president of the University of New Hampshire and is currently vice-president of the University of Illinois. He has served on many educational advisory boards, including several for universities in Africa. He has contributed articles to political science and education journals. Johnson believes that racial agitation, because it is based on genuine grievances, may be the most important force in the university today for agitation and reform. He argues that although universities cannot be held totally responsible for cultural disadvantage or for the entire task of change and reform, their record of racial and economic discrimination is evident, and they have an obligation to take a leadership role in bringing about change.

RACIAL AGITATION hits the universities at their vulnerable points. University people, generally speaking, have a conscience which is already sensitized and perhaps guilt-ridden on racial matters. They are so given to learning-by-discourse that they will endure infinite verbal abuse with politeness. They are so hostile to the use of force where ideas are involved —even seemingly ridiculous ideas—that they give cover and sanctuary which the outside public would not long tolerate. Aware of their role as social critics, they are reluctant to seem to be found imperceptive or derelict in their duty. In assessing student discipline, they are sensitized to individual infractions, not mass defiance. Torn between conscience and reason, they may dissemble in response to "non-negotiable demands,"

Reprinted by permission from Elden L. Johnson, *From Riot to Reason* (Urbana: University of Illinois Press, 1971), chap. 4.

75

which leads later to accusations of bad faith. Finally, some university group with influence, if not authority, will almost certainly find its conscience so pricked by any—literally any —appeal in the name of racial justice that serious division in the academic community ensues. Racial problems, in other words, top all current campus issues in their capacity to put strains on the creaking joints of the academic machine, although it would ill become the university to be less sensitive, humane, and responsive.

The siege of the universities may, therefore, reach its turning point on racial grounds. All campus dissidents have always faced the twin questions of issue and method, and the efficacy of the latter for the former. Unlike some of the would-be revolutionaries whose strategies outrun their issues, the blacks have genuine grievances. They are left to argue about method. Too astute to be diverted or used by leftist elements, yet frustrated by conventional methods, the blacks have paralleled the major dissidents in escalating the methodology of attack. As a result, the militants soon looked moderate enough to lead. Sit-ins turned into building seizures. Non-negotiable demands became popular. One-way "communication"—the ultimate—gained acceptance. Speeches and publications of calculated insults and of filthy language, allegedly purified by ghetto-origin, became common currency. One kind of militancy polarized another kind, and each accused the other of racism. It became a foregone conclusion that eventually the extremes would overreach themselves, unwittingly bringing the university to terms with its own permissiveness and indecision.

The spiraling madness reached its apogee when the most militant, sometimes in groups and sometimes individually, appeared on several campuses with rifles, pistols, and knives. The academic nadir came when university communities, although fortunately only momentarily, responded with confused indecision and debated whether even this was beyond the pale, the rules, or the law. This ratiocination soon tripped over common sense. The nature of a university is not that obscure. Openness has to have bounds. From this pragmatic lesson, universities may have found a new watershed. They may now be able to set some bounds. They may now better learn how to outlaw destruction without throttling dissent. Indeed they may now be helped to set the conditions for institutional survival and thus to get on with the reforms which can commend themselves to university men who have surely now become socially sensitized.

This turn-about in university response to the "shut it down" extremist strategy is only one of several changes which larger numbers of black students on campus have precipitated. The catalytic influence comes from the confrontation of "the black problem" and "the white problem" in a community dedicated to reasoned change.

Universities were the scene of the first big break in racial desegregation in the South. Everywhere throughout the country, they are still the scene of agitation in race relations. They are the cutting edge of reform, although by no means always of their choice. Universities are being asked to pay a disproportionate share of society's debt to the black race. Demands that belong elsewhere are dumped at the university's door, along with legitimate claims.

But be that as it may, universities have sown the whirlwind —generally without malice but surely with colossal indifference. Their record in educating black youth is scandalous. If black youth were not often enough "qualified" for admission, the universities, as vaunted social critics, said little enough about it and did even less. As authoritative spokesmen for education, universities rarely drew public conclusions from the appalling statistics of racial disparity in university enrollments, reflecting, as it did, the alarming cumulative effect of disadvantage heaped upon disadvantage, from kindergarten to campus.

Figures for 1967 show that blacks comprised slightly more than two per cent of the enrollment in predominantly white institutions. By 1969, they were six per cent in all institutions, whereas they made up twelve per cent of the college-eligible age group and a like proportion of the total population. The progressive nature of this conspicuous disadvantage is shown in graduate enrollment: blacks comprised only one per cent in 1967 and less than that figure for doctoral candidates in 1969, with only two per cent in law and slightly better in medicine. These figures obscure still grimmer facts:

1. One-half of all black students are in predominantly black institutions.
2. Consequently half are in institutions with limited occupational coverage, still with heavy emphasis on teacher preparation.
3. In law, engineering, nursing, and education, predominantly black institutions are still the major producers of black professionals.
4. There are more foreign students than native blacks in the predominately white American universities.
5. In predominately white universities, there is little correlation between their black enrollment and their proximity to black concentration of youth: universities in cities where blacks make up a quarter, a third, or half of the population often show black enrollments of a fiftieth, a twentieth, or rarely a tenth of the total enrollment.

All this is a shocking social commentary. The disparity is quite beyond the bounds of rational defense.

Emphasis needs be placed on this as a *social* commentary

first and a *university* commentary secondarily. What the university could do, by the time the cumulative effects of cultural disadvantage reached the thirteenth grade, was limited; but what the university did do, even so, was not socially responsive.

For balance and accuracy, mitigating circumstances should be noted. No one can prove that most universities were, in the past, intentionally operating on racial lines. The evidence is quite the opposite. They were operating on economic lines— inertly, unwittingly, merely admitting the youth whose economic status had brought them through high school with the required academic marks. The proof of black discrimination by inadvertence is shown by the same fate suffered by youth in similar economic circumstances, including other minority groups such as Puerto Ricans. It is also shown by the ready admission of foreign non-whites armed with scholarships or possessing independent means. In other words, the university record in educating poor youth, like black youth, has been scandalous also. On economic inequality as a deterrent to education, however, the universities have not been entirely silent, although the academic conscience has still seemed remarkably somnolent until recently. Now, monetary equalization of educational opportunity is the latest and most popular educational reform. Almost, but not quite, everybody embraces it, at least in theory. The rationale is still economic and not racial, although the black dimension has often become explicit.

Another mitigating circumstance: it is beyond the power of the university, in one, four, or even five years to undo what society, the home, and the lower schools have done in eighteen or twenty years. And there is no reason why the university alone should be saddled with the total task. What the black wants, ought to have, and must get is the opportunity and education which will make race irrelevant and compensatory treatment unnecessary at the time of university entrance. He will not be free and equal until that day arrives. Helping it arrive is a legitimate and urgent university objective—indeed for all youth regardless of race.

Meanwhile, black youth have brought their identity crisis to the university campus. All factions are there—the same factions that split the black race elsewhere in society. Some want revolution; some will settle for reform. Some want symbols; some want substance. Some bank on black capitalism; some advocate world socialism. Equally divergent are the proposed strategies: some for gradualism, some for instant remedy. Agreement is on victory, not on its meaning; and some factions provide no base for communication or accommodation because they choose to "outblack" all other blacks. Unfortunately, in the current balance of forces, the militancy of the streets has come to the campus. The same militancy mans the bullhorns, talks tough, cows the moderates, and stridently issues ultimatums. It is often hard to see any other image of negritude on campus at present. In contrast, however, when concrete actionable programs are under discussion, different priorities and philosophies arise to confound university officials who learn that there is no "black" solution to the so-called black problems.

Nevertheless, of all the forces shaking up the traditional university and shaping reform, the "black problem" may prove to be the greatest. The potency does not lie in superior leadership or strategy, but rather in the fact that the problem is stuck in our conscience, persistently remains, and has to be absorbed somehow. Its festering, its abrasiveness, its excesses only give dramatic point to nagging awareness. Racial injustice, fully recognized but only partially mitigated, is a leaden shadow which shortens the stature of everyone in the intellectual community.

By its haunting presence, the black problem challenges the traditional assumption that the university is a liberal institution. That university self-image will have to be reexamined. If general education liberalized and liberated, why had nobody asked whom it liberated and why not others? If learning made for social mobility, why had no attention been paid to who went up and who never got on the escalator at all? If the university held a monopoly on entry into all the major professions, how equitably had it doled out opportunity and how well had its resulting graduates served all segments of American society? If the academic community claimed the high prerogative of social criticism, how well had it anticipated the greatest American crisis of the twentieth century and how had it responded in its own house?

The inevitable university answer, "Race is irrelevant," only compounds the indictment. Race *ought* to be irrelevant, but was it? What in fact *did* happen? It is the practice, not the theory, which is most researchable; and universities are supposed to be good at research. How liberal is an institution which knows so little about its own illiberality?

At still another point, the black presence challenges the university as no other criticism has. It challenges the idea that an institution of higher education derives its uniqueness from being a meritocracy. Merit, yes, but by what standard? Grades? Tests? Conventionality? The challenge is twofold: whether there are not other equally or more relevant criteria which should at least be combined with time-honored tradition and whether the right objective is being served. Another appealing and competing value has appeared on the scene: equality. As a result, the social dimension of equality now has to be added to the individual dimension of merit. Awareness is at last fixed on the circularity of confining the system to those who already fit the system, thus educating the risk-free.

The raucous black demand, perhaps "non-negotiable," that blacks should be admitted to universities (generally or in black studies) "without regard to grades" challenges the other conventional extreme of "with regard to little or nothing but grades." It reshuffles the criteria. If a university, for example, promises to take half of its entering freshmen from minority groups in its immediate urban neighborhood, not from the highest-scored applicants but from a cross-section of those who have made the high school hurdle, what has it done to its quality? And to its standards? The black problem rudely asks the real meaning of "quality" and "standards." Quality to what end? Standards by whose standards: those of an egalitarian society, of possessors of talent, or of academic guardians of "the system"? Standards set by students admitted with an ever-rising level of past academic achievement (witness entering classes from the top five percentiles!), by norms in the discipline, or by predicted performance level in eventual employment? In fact, do standards consciously relate to any criteria which are explicitly meaningful to individuals or to society? Forced attention to these questions has demonstrated that there are indeed answers and combinations of considerations all too rarely examined heretofore. The new appeal of "open admissions" has put even the elitist universities on the defensive. As a result, the composition of student bodies—racially and economically, generally and in particular institutions—is undergoing revolutionary change.

Whether by black "demands" or by mere black presence, the ubiquitous race problem on campus also asks how the university harmonizes its vaunted universality with its white-European limitations and its neglect of much larger populations and much larger world areas inhabited by people of color. How modern and relevant is a center of higher learning which is so slow in heavily supplementing the transmission of a single culture, however great it is—in a country of rich subcultures and in a world of different and problem-creating peoples, both abounding in unparalleled opportunities for research and public service, to say nothing of the implications for the curriculum? University reassessment along these lines may immeasurably enrich the humanities and social sciences. The "black perspective" is not adequate either, but it will behoove the university to embrace that perspective and many other perspectives which collectively illuminate all humanity. If universities are to continue to be culture-bound, recognizing that cultural priorities are inevitable, they will be the stronger for having consciously examined *why* and consciously determined the subcultural mix.

The blacks, supported by basic justice which "the establishment" must feel and eventually recognize, can make a university impact which ideological radicals can never muster. Even the excesses carry a message if not lost in the backlash. Therefore, the greatest query of all which implicitly faces the university concerns its purpose, mission, and justification. This goes back to fundamentals in a salutary manner not recently seen. But if the "salvation" provided by higher education is *in fact* denied to a huge segment of the American population —the disadvantaged by both income and race—the real purpose of colleges and universities is called into question. Doing what it takes to survive the system until degree-conferral, without questioning "what it takes," or how to get in, is hardly an answer. Do any concessions have to be made to serving human welfare, maximizing productivity (utilizing human resources otherwise wasted), fulfilling individual capacity, or even producing interracial comity? To what should the intellectualization be harnessed? The answer for higher education in total may be different from the answer for a particular university, but the time is obviously at hand for clearer answers for both.

Speaking of institutional variety, the predominantly black colleges and universities are in danger of being forgotten in the anxiety about "doing something for the education of blacks." The desired leverage is in the predominantly white institutions. The issue can be drawn more convincingly there. The racist-looking confrontations have to be there. So that is where the attention flows. That is where the "opening up" must take place and where access to superior quality can be gained; but the facts of where black students actually are, and will long be, should not be overlooked. Unless revolutionary change takes place there, the black higher educational problem will be only half solved. Aiding black institutions could indeed perpetuate segregation, but it is too late either to begin *de novo* or to go on waiting for the ideal time for help. Remedy seems to lie in the determination of institutional leaders, donors, trustees, and government *not* to perpetuate segregation. It is impoverishment, not new resources, that will obviate change.

Black institutions, in general, are unstable; teachers are underpaid; the best students tend to be lost to other institutions; libraries are deficient; curricula do not match the spectrum of modern careers; research funds are absent; and funds for public service are virtually nonexistent. Yet these institutions have two great potentials for which modern society is eagerly looking: experience in educating the deprived and special access to persons in special need of public services. Why the federal government has been so slow in detecting these capacities and capitalizing on them is a question which appears to have, at best, an unsatisfactory answer. If it is because the institutions, in all candor, are not very good, that is precisely why the same government *is* helping universities overseas. It is hard to think of another illustration of compensatory justice which is so overdue as drastically stepped-up federal support for black colleges and universities.

The story of the black catalytic force in university life is not complete without consideration also of the current excesses of militants who so overstate their case that only a predetermined reply—in the negative—is possible. This is the opposite of the appeals to justice and conscience, coupled with drama and insistence, which have given the blacks success beyond their on-campus members. The university must be prepared to decode much of the gross language in which militant communications are couched, often for another audience. Something sometimes comes through. A grievance is indeed there. A horrendous case may turn out to be not horrendous but admittedly beyond defense. A long-standing practice may show up in new light, stripped of its presumed validity. But after all the decoding, translating, and discounting have taken place, many of the militant "demands" threaten not to reform but to destroy the university. Therefore, sorting out the gradations of workability and the clarity of dangers is not an easy task.

Criteria presumably should not be different from those applied to other "demands" for university reform, whatever the origin and the subject. A few obvious questions might be asked, not because there will be clear answers but because likely consequences need to be perceived and weighed.

Is the proposal compatible with the university's mission or inimical to it? As stated above, conceptions of mission are being rethought; but even so, beyond some degree of change (difficult as it may be to determine, except at the extreme, and particularly in the light of a legitimate public service role) the university ceases to be what it professes and becomes another kind of social institution—maybe a prep school, a welfare agency, a community recreation center, or an indoctrination authority. Demands have sometimes been made which make no sense by any reasonable or even strained interpretation of what a university really is.

Is the university in a position to exercise responsibility for the acts involved? Is it in fact, and not someone else, in charge? Some of the earliest proposals for Afro-American studies programs clearly sought university implementation, including finance, while shifting actual control elsewhere, sometimes even to student-chosen "directors" whose names would not be divulged. Permitting black cadres to recruit fellow blacks with decisions on both admissions and scholarships is another "demand" which negates the university's authority and public trust. Having Black Panthers write black history is no more acceptable than having John Birchers write American history. Unless the university preserves both control of its own affairs and use of its good name, it can easily find itself not embracing a clean purpose but locked into an ulterior one—to strengthen a faction, to buy an ally, or to injure less-vocal blacks.

Can the proposal be universalized? Would it make sense if applied to everyone, or similar groups, including other minority groups? Can it be replicated? Rigid quota proposals get into trouble at this point. Does twelve per cent for blacks mean X per cent for Puerto Ricans, Y per cent for Japanese-Americans, and so on ad infinitum? Is this by colleges and departments, too? Likewise, can and should housing along racial lines be provided for other races or all races? And can ethnic curricula be farmed out to all ethnic groups? The university must be aware that the sword has another side, which may do injury to someone else.

Is the proposed change compatible with the peculiar purpose of that which is being reformed (or if not, is the new purpose indeed more appropriate)? The university may ask that question when its rule-enforcement body considers a demand for student amnesty for acts not yet committed; or when it receives an ultimatum to strip and tether the campus security force; or when it is told to divest its endowment of all "investments in evil" anywhere in the world.

No magic answers pop up for these questions, but many implications do. Every course of action has its price and requires its defense in the court of ultimate consequences. Can the university ultimately live with its decision, in its full flowering and certain replication?

Answers would be less negative if the demands were less extreme. But race on campus, in its current articulated form, is extremist; it is sometimes itself racist. Therein lies two ugly dangers. Both are escape hatches, plausible excuses, and ways around responsible action. Universities should be too wise and too humane to seize them.

The first danger is the "easy out" of pointing the finger elsewhere for remedy. The university can readily say, and has sometimes said, that the black admissions problem belongs to the vocational school or junior college; the ghetto problem belongs to government; the black employment problem belongs to industry; and on and on. What the university needs to do is to stop asking what its jurisdiction is and begin asking how it can help solve the problem. It may indeed be ill-suited, or not suited at all, for direct attack on many of the problems, but with its vaunted competence in all human knowledge, it can hardly say that it has nothing to contribute, with whatever degree of indirection is fitting (e.g., consulting instead of doing, preparing teachers rather than teaching, educating practitioners instead of practicing).

The temptation to irresponsibility, however, can best be seen by confining attention to the extension of educational opportunities to blacks. Whose job is this? Until now, it has been either unrecognized or the answer has been shuttled back and forth among educational institutions, with responsibility coming to rest nowhere, either individually or collectively. The problem has fallen through the cracks of institutional self-images and jurisdictions. Meanwhile no one can deny that *society* has a problem and a responsibility—a problem to be met somewhere, somehow. The public sector of that responsibility will have to rely on public educational institutions. It behooves such institutions, therefore, to consult and map strategy, with appropriate division of labor, to get the job done. Who takes the lead—government, university, junior college, vocational school—is immaterial; but the university is derelict in its duty if it waits for initiative elsewhere. Furthermore, it is in the university's highest self-interest to initiate action. As a college official plaintively remarked recently, the college is now presented with a bill of claims for three hundred years of black grievances. Whatever part of the bill is to be recognized and however to be paid, it will have to be shared among a host of social institutions according to their peculiar missions and special competencies. The university is, however, fitted for a leadership role.

The second danger lies in the accommodative mood of the contemporary university. It may let the black militant have his segregation—with incalculable cost to posterity, and particularly to other blacks. Remember that the universities once set the pattern in the rights of blacks. What irony if an American version of apartheid were someday to be historically attributed to the universities! And what irony for the sophomoric Bantu who might too late be surprised at how many whites are willing to "recognize" his negritude.

Every study rates racial concerns as a primary cause of academic unrest, and this is a problem which has a clear-cut campus component—about which something can be done. Therefore, race as seen on campus persistently raises questions, including fundamental, philosophical ones, which universities can no longer avoid and cannot answer except by better understanding themselves and their need for reform. Hopefully, history will eventually record that campus extremism represented attention-getting attacks on gross social ills at least then ameliorated. But in the final analysis, the most important historical judgment will be on what universities did, not with their students, but with their potential leadership for solving the problems which youthful conscience had identified.

Ghetto Blacks and College Policy

BY JACK J. CARDOSO

Jack J. Cardoso obtained his Ph.D. from the University of Wisconsin and has taught at Chico and Hayward State Colleges in California. Active in the Urban League's SEEK Program, he is currently teaching black history at the New York State University College at Buffalo. Maintaining that black students view the white colleges as the hostile enemy, Cardoso argues that administrators have refused to take a positive stand on many of the demands of the students. Instead, overwhelmed by guilt, they make no rational responses to students who are looking for direction.

THERE ARE MANY ISSUES of irrelevancy on college campuses today, but regarding young Black students, two of these irrelevancies stand out. One is that traditional college society and all it infers is irrelevent to the Blacks. The other is the irrelevancy of their college experience to those Blacks whose personal world has been alien to life outside the Negro community of poverty. The two problems come together violently when ghetto Black students find themselves being patterned by what they regard to be the template of white racism. The conceptions which Blacks have of white society at large are narrowed dramatically on campus.

The confines of the ghetto offer to the poor an isolated security not available or even discernible in the large society. The inhabitant of the ghetto has a unique awareness of status

Reprinted by permission from *Liberal Education* LV (Oct., 1969): 363–72.

in his neighborhood. He knows where to live, where to buy, and how to exist in any situation. His joys and sorrows, faith and distrust, victories and defeats, are shared experiences despite a general absence of personal relationships. Before the world without, ghetto dwellers take care of their own. For Blacks to find themselves pulled or pushed into the outside world is to suffer a traumatic experience. This experience is both frightening and confounding in its complexities, and out of the challenge there develops a natural tendency to withdraw to the comfort of certainty that the ghetto offers. And should factors of geography, ego, futility, or even the nature of the challenge itself, make withdrawal unfeasible or impossible, then the creation of an extension of the ghetto society becomes natural and ethical. "Getting it together" and "doing your thing" assume the outlines of a subcultural group, the base being the common experience of Black ghetto life. The majority of Black youths share in the ghetto experience, and those who have little in common with it are ostracized until they accept the ethic or perform an exercise in "mea culpism" for not being part of the Black ancestral "home." These Blacks guiltily embrace what they imagine must be indigenous to their own blackness and their reaction is comparable to the guilt felt by comparable whites when confronted with the absolutes that racism entails. Middle-class Blacks and sensitive whites compromise both principle and integrity by lending their energies to making reality out of fantasy. Middling Blacks are easily victimized when the ghetto majority holds a superior position by virtue of their number on campus. This factor of number rather than organizational expertise dominates when Blacks with common experiences draw together to confront the "hostile" world of the college. The phrase, "hostile white society," goes beyond radical rhetoric; it is rather the wail of a fearful minority coming together toward a security that derives from being with their own through a lifetime and more.

The situation of challenge which the college represents and which compels such withdrawal creates ambivalence, for education holds the possibility of new opportunity. However, the college represents a greater reality than many Black youths are willing to confront for several reasons. The college can be a transitory experience, that is, by failing the student it can be withdrawn at short notice. Also, for better or worse, the college is still a crucible of competition. Ghetto Blacks too often tend to believe that any competition with whites in education will be inherently unequal and that on present terms they are unable to cope with the outside world which the college represents. For Blacks, such confrontation becomes superconfrontation, for to them college in American life is traditionally the special privilege of children of the whitest of American society; college students are the cream of the middle and upper economic constituency whose understanding of the ghetto, let alone Blacks, does not exist. On the other hand, when Black ghetto youths—lured by handsome stipends, impelled by fantasies of what college life is like, harassed by high school counselors, and even badgered by "recruiting" vanguards from "reforming" colleges—hit the campus, they suffer what may be termed cultural shock for they are now in a milieu totally alien to their backgrounds. The middle America, about which they feel rather than know, represents an impregnable and forbidding frontier to ghetto Blacks; and the campus, that bedrock foundation of the middle class, is believed to be the instrument of white racism.

Black collegians therefore resort to the mystique of being denizens of ghettodom. White students, upon first contact with Blacks, are often enamored and titillated by the new association. The proximity to a culture as distant to their own as theirs is to Blacks, intensifies white interest. However, this infatuation heightens the anxiety for Blacks who both resent and delight in their newly discovered uniqueness. Temporarily the new relationships are cultivated and exploited, but the demands of scholastic life soon take precedence over mere social intercourse. Familiarity with the procedural structure of the college allows white students to follow the old patterns of college existence while Blacks are uncertain and confused by the general democratic ethic of the academic community and are unable fully to comprehend the new reality. The functions of college living become real in relatively devastating ways: Blacks are thrust into competition with scholastically motivated and aggressive whites and, at the same time, they are confronted with academic semantics and content which are unknown to the ghetto at large. Further, white students, who are geared toward prescribed degree goals channel their energies toward securing their own reality and structuring their social life to match. In contrast, the anxiety margins of Black youths are quickly exhausted as the impact of college life is felt, and retreat becomes the immediate reaction—retreat to a community of themselves and a reality with which they are totally familiar. There is a natural getting together in a kind of superficial ghetto within the ivy. To the Blacks the college has become proof of a white hostility they have been trained to guard against. "Doing your thing," both curricular and extracurricular to the normal affairs of college living, becomes a necessity.

Withdrawal from the traditional business of higher education then demands the institutionalizing of rationalization: Blacks are to determine that the colleges are not relevant to Blacks; colleges do not have enough Blacks as teachers; African courses teach from the white man's viewpoint, or, African

History is not relevant to Afro-American History; slavery is a white "thing" and therefore has nothing to do with Blacks; only Black professors can teach Black subjects since whites can never know a Black "thing"; colleges don't know or care anything about the real world of the ghetto. Empathy among student Blacks brings about a further escape to "soul" which becomes a part of the mystique of blackness and seen as an esoteric quality of Blacks alone, communicable only among Blacks. Soul courses such as "Soul Foods," "The Ghetto Experience" or "The Genius of Poverty" and indulgent, ego-supporting subjects such as "Black Revolutionaries" and "The Life and Thought of Malcolm X" are conjured up to go with "Soul Art," "Soul Music," "Soul Drama" and "The Black Renaissance"—all of which are packaged into the new reality of a Black Studies major.

This newly found reality is not rejected totally by the colleges which, although bureaucratically reluctant to change themselves, are liberally susceptible to amelioration. Administrators and faculty tend to accept the new mission within the context of tradition. However, even total acceptance of Black desires does not bring satisfaction to the Blacks. Uncertain of their new involvement in the "hostile" college and longing for an honorable retreat to the certainty of ghetto society, they find their insecurity intensified even further. They recognize that, beyond the Black Studies major they have created, three-fourths of the Black students' training is to be spent studying standard subject matter. The old confrontation is ever present. Thus the academic subculture must again be enlarged in order to anesthetize itself against future anxiety. The immediacies rather than the ends of college education hold priority. The enlargement takes the form of demands for "Black Colleges" which are viewed by Blacks as being autonomous and ethical entities, providing an extension of the ghetto security and a sinecure against competitive involvement with what has now become an oppressive white educational world. To fortify these demands, Blacks push for open admission of all Blacks regardless of potential and, to maintain the cadre already present, there is the cry for removal of failing grades or even for eradication of any and all systems of determining performance. When Blacks run afoul of campus regulations autonomy is immediately claimed: the academic ghetto, just as the ghetto outside, reacts directly and often violently to intrusions on its sphere. Traditional faculty-student judicial boards are declared unqualified to judge Blacks, and the new mystique of uniqueness—of difference—is honored by antiauthoritarian white students and by confused and casual liberal faculty members. This exercise in Black escape is aided, abetted, and fortified by white guilt which interprets the acceptance of Black desires as a means by which whites can exculpate their ancestral sins. White college men and women have literally wept over their "responsibility" for segregation, slavery, and Black emasculation. Idealistic youths, caught in the finalities that graduation and selective service represent, also join the issue with their own general protests against anything representative of the Establishment and strive to achieve status with the literal children of the downtrodden.

Perhaps a more illusory insecurity for Blacks on the campuses is that concerning sex and the exploration of it. The white college world is essentially male-oriented. The faculty can be considered dominantly male; athletics, party life, conversation, fraternities and student enrollment are masculine-dominated. Women become the object of discriminating cultivation by males while girls, in turn, become aware of the first real possibility of worthwhile matrimony. Despite the protestations of emancipated coeds, living and loving and possible marriage are enduring as a trinity; colleges provide a more interesting alternative to their local high schools and neighborhoods. Black enrollments also tend to lean toward the masculine; thus the field for sexual indulgence is proscribed in several ways. Black males are products of a general society maternally dominated and the attitudes of Black males toward females can be traced to the matriarchal condition of the home. The dearth of Black coeds limits the possibilities of normal sexual exploration. The predominantly white student population is traditionally schooled against interracial sexual companionship by social mores and by lack of historical association. A compounding factor is that many colleges are located in communities without large numbers of "townie" Blacks with whom association would be natural. Furthermore, in colleges which are within cities having concentrations of Blacks, the ego of "college Blacks" sets them apart intellectually from their ghetto counterparts who may never go to college. A final problem surrounds the ability of Blacks from the ghetto to relate socially with middle- and upper-class whites, especially women, who have been regarded as privileged persons in the white America.

This sexual insecurity compels Black males to seek release from their frustrations in many standard ways. The adoption of or taking on the trappings of sexuality becomes general, and many of these are exercises in super-sexual fantasy. These include the pseudo-harem relationship in Afro-American Clubs where Black sisters are assigned positions inferior to their Black "warrior" brothers, a la tribal custom or at least a concept of it. The wearing of phallic symbols such as carvings, bones, bullet casings, chains, earrings, pencils and objects in the hair, or symbolic "guerilla" gear—berets, fatigues, field jackets, and leatherware—all contribute to the creation of a distorted masculine image. The cultivation of facial hair completes the "new manliness" which is then framed in a stern, aloof, sullen countenance, all providing a superficial shield against reality. This blatant reversal of form in adornments from the faddish "fly" gear of the ghetto is an extension of the same problem and to some extent is an exercise in personal therapy. The infatuation with the assertion of masculinity and physical competence by young Blacks is deemed necessary in confronting the hostile world of confident whites. This overtness is attested to further by Black attitudes toward Black women. Comments in the possessive are the rule: "our women" and "protection of our sisters" are allusions both to male dominance (a new status for Black males) and to historical imaginings that female Blacks have always been objects of sexual exploitation by "immoral" whites. In reality, social relations between white males and Black females on the campus seldom exist. On the other hand, white females who are asserting their own independence and illusory daring, often avail themselves of Black male companionship. However, the Blacks then suffer the guilt of deserting their own, and the maintenance of the purity of their "own women" becomes even more important. Black male anxiety is further heightened by the eventuality that, though Black women have been inured to male desertion in the ghetto society, they will not be willing to remain a step to the rear as their own horizons are broadened by higher learning.

To Blacks, college is an almost unbelievable actuality. To them, colleges in the United States are relatively the most democratic and open societies in the world, inhabited by a majority class which indulges itself in everything imagination allows. To them, faculty and administrators are virtual enigmas who occupy amorphous positions of authority and appear at prescribed times for prescribed occasions—classes, meetings, forums, registration, special events, awards, etc. Yet they are masters without mandate. The liberal training they have received is the basis for their role in the superior society on campus, the traditional concept of which holds that authoritarian notions are inimicable to academic life. They are the articulators of past and future, but escape the present. The reinforcing of tradition in the future is both the thrust of their teaching and the essence of their own training. For them the flowering of intellectuality demands an atmosphere free of restraint. Yet this insular quality of academe contributes both strength and fragility, for when the campus is faced with unstructured radical confrontations its weaknesses are exposed.

The difficulty of colleges in seeing the options available in reacting to Black students is attributable to their inexperience in handling physical expressions of social antagonism. Ironically, this lack of experience is a cherishable reminder of the spirit of freedom that has personified most of American academic history. This open and democratic society is tested and exploited by young Blacks living by values learned in the ghetto. They are uncertain of, and thus unwilling to accept, the possibility that a college is not hostile. To them, the college is simply the most vulnerable of what they believe to be white institutions of oppression; and in its vulnerability they see a distorted hope that all white society is weak, fearful and inferior. Such fires of hostility are fed by the notion that the campuses are training schools for white racism, and any education dispensed is glibly tossed off as being irrelevant to the world of Blacks on the ground that it is designed simply to maintain the white culture. This is again an exercise in escape. The unfortunate thing about such fantasies is that they lead capable Black students into easy rationalizations. While there is no end to the number of Blacks who have shown that knowledge is universal, the motivations of individuals are not necessarily the motivations of groups, and collective products of the ghetto structure have yet to resolve their problems of insecurity and aspiration.

Black students would have it both ways in their pursuit of security and instant culture. Though decrying curriculums as irrelevant, in the same voice they insist that Blacks are not only as capable as whites but, rather, superior! The mystical "Black Thing" is waved like a sword of conscience, and whites become contrite at being unable to comprehend it and blame themselves for ostensibly suppressing it. Such a facile resort to the "Super-Black" position becomes oddly serious on the loose, fragile, liberal-oriented campus. Logic and rationality become secondary to the anxiety of impending crisis. Harried whites and middle-class Blacks become addled if not confounded, for the dimensions of absurdity appear immeasurable. A kind of intellectual masochism is indulged by many whites who actually compete to accept notions that Blacks, if they so desire, can readily comprehend the "soul" of Greek philosophy, of Shakespeare, or of Goethe, but that whites can never truly know a "Black Thing." The geography of this irrationality is boundless and the character it assumes, fantastic; for instance, the wafting of odors of "soul food" over a largely white audience during the reading of Black poetry and prose, or obtaining sensationalist Black militant speakers who deliver packaged contradictions excoriating their white audiences who are titillated by the verbal whiplash.[1]

The social tragedy which lies at the base of Black student thinking could be doubled should ghetto conjecture about colleges become a reality. An authoritarian reaction becomes fearfully inevitable to the extent that Blacks persist in the

[1] One example can be found in the article by Gerald Weales, "The Day LeRoi Jones spoke on Penn Campus—What Were the Blacks Doing in the Balcony?" *New York Times Magazine,* May 4, 1969.

notion of Fanon that "hate makes evil legitimate."[2] The indulgent society of the college which has been tolerant of everything short of murder is in danger of being deserted by the hitherto uninvolved and worshipful society which makes colleges possible. Legislatures, trustees, administrative councils, and the violence-saturated public at large stir restlessly; the demand for an expedient solution appears imminent. Such expediency can take the form of demands for the resignation of the agents of the college and their replacement by creatures of reaction, the withholding of funds, the use of uniformed force, the foreclosure of programs still in infancy, and overall strictures on the freedom of academic inquiry. The larger society, reviled by the brutal sensationalism of student reformers, will not pause to distinguish between Blacks and whites nor their differing desires for reform. To the ordinary citizen the cost of the cure takes priority over the genesis of the disorder.

Within the campus itself, administration and faculty members taking accusatory stances might turn on one another (and already have) to the detriment of teaching, research, and the affairs of the college generally. In this respect there is considerable evidence that individuals from both areas have used campus uprisings to serve mean ends. In a desperate desire for the tranquility of the past, colleges may desert entirely the field of credibility, distort the academic structure, and succumb to the view that rationality is relative. For a college to accept any proposition simply to preserve the campus would be an exercise in competitive absurdity. Another eventuality, already evident on some campuses, is that administrators may use Black enrollments as leverage to secure larger budget allocations. They may also accept lower grade admission re-

[2] Franz Fanon, *The Wretched of the Earth* (New York: Grove Press, 1968).

quirements without faculty consultation, establish new criteria for grants-in-aid, and funnel off funds from established academic areas to feed hastily constructed, and often ill-conceived, public relations oriented projects.

The greatest tragedy, however, would be the creation of an oppressive academic climate. Colleges must accept the confrontation with the totality of Black involvement, and its "demands" must be received with the rationality that liberal minds pride themselves in exercising. Should the college prove to be as hostile as Blacks believe, then irrationality becomes reason. The present generation of Black collegians perhaps represents the vanguard of this nation's primary hope for the creation of a new society. When Blacks find colleges to be legitimately open and secure, not the simple agents of a believed racist society, the message will become clear in the consciousness of the ghetto-poor. Thus the mission of the college is to resolve the ambivalence of Blacks who desire the security of a simplistic neighborhood and yet crave success. Colleges need to provide Blacks with something positive to tell their fellows should they return to the ghetto. Education is not in the business of preaching hate and inspiring social antagonism. Further, colleges cannot indulge the anxious by establishing narrow programs devoted to apartheid. The sense of all that learning entails must be felt by all the students.

But the colleges must also accept change. Anachronistic major fields and similar vocationally oriented programs need phasing out; the concept of an open curriculum beyond the freshman or sophomore year would present no threat to education. Indeed it would liberate the campus from the maze of divisions, programs, and institutes which are often mere decaying duchies. The significant challenge to the college is that of discerning between the credible and incredible that Black reform often represents. The failure to defend against the absurd is as evil as to purvey it. Young ghetto Blacks insist on a stand being taken by the college, for the ghetto community lives with threats and absolutes. Among Blacks, order is both craved and disrupted; leaders and spokesmen change quickly; demands are confused and even altered during presentation; whites are cultivated and rejected, often simultaneously; threats are overstated; and the nervous counting of numbers represents legitimacy. Even when a college accepts demands, Black students boggle as they stumble over the rationalization of their original belligerency and the results of their insurgency. What has occurred is that the college has failed to play the part of finding where it's at by simply admitting it doesn't know. The young radical who offers himself on the warhead of revolt fully expects to be mangled, but campus officials are too worried and compromised to be aware of this ethic of revolution. Failure to react in a preconceived way is evidence to the street-mind that an enemy is weak, which in turn makes the cause good. Thus the extremes are enlarged, each act becoming more irrational—and when there is an absence of positive action from the college—absurdity becomes legitimate and chaos becomes style.

What we have here are the politics of extremes with only one side playing. The sad fact of this game of progressive "chicken" is the failure of both sides to understand the nature of the other; the colleges are especially at fault because, by superior knowledge and training, there should at least be some comprehension of the nature of the contest. Everyone, and especially the insecure poor of the Black ghetto, respects the taking of a position. Colleges must establish for themselves the stand they will assume. Black students want something positive which deals with Blacks, something that will become a lasting part of the college. Though some administrators have accepted this in theory, they do not realize that Blacks do not readily believe or even understand budget semantics and curriculum jargon. Even Black professors take a jaundiced view of college commitments to Black education as can be seen in their peripatetic search for tenure rather than simple challenge and opportunity. College officials must literally "put up" in two ways: instituting viable courses dealing with the Negro and dealing with extremism in a positive manner. The outrageous must be ostracized. Order will not come from within the student body, for students are socially and psychologically unequipped to deal with their own. When our rebels see for themselves that colleges are sincere and secure, then the business of college life can resume. It would be too great an extension of the absurd to hear again the words of the Black youths of Watts, standing amid the carnage of dozens of dead and with their neighborhood in ashes: "We won: we won because we made them pay attention to us."[3]

[3] Martin Luther King, Jr., *Where Do We Go From Here?* (New York: Harper & Row, 1967), p. 112.

Black Studies: Trouble Ahead

BY EUGENE D. GENOVESE

Eugene D. Genovese, chairman of the History Department at the University of Rochester, was born in Brooklyn, New York, received his B.A. from Brooklyn College and Ph.D. from Columbia University. He has taught at the Polytechnic Institute of Brooklyn, Rutgers, Sir George Williams College, and Yale University. A Marxist, Genovese is probably the best known admirer of Ulrich B. Phillips among young Southern historians. The most widely read of Genovese's several books is The Political Economy of Slavery. *Contrary to the view of Pentony, Genovese claims that there are several black ideologies and that all of them should be represented in a Black Studies program. If one black group is allowed to exclude other black groups or whites from participation in the programs, Genovese fears that this will lead to campus-wide purges of "reactionaries," "liberals," and "revolutionaries" as the power of these groups vacillates. Genovese agrees, however, with Hare and Jordan that Black Studies programs can forge the black intelligentsia needed in the black community.*

NO PROBLEM so agitates the campuses today as that posed by the growing pressure for black studies programs and departments. The agitation presents special dangers since it can be, and sometimes is, opportunistically manipulated by the nihilist factions of the radical white student movement. For the most part, black students have shown considerable restraint in dealing with dubious white allies and have given strong indication of being much more interested in reforming the universities than in burning them down. The black student

Reprinted by permission from *The Atlantic Monthly* CCXXII (June, 1969): 37–41.

movement, like some parts of the white radical student movement and very much unlike others, represents an authentic effort by young people to take a leading role in the liberation of an oppressed people and, as such, exhibits impressive seriousness and developing sophistication. The political forms that the agitation takes and the deep frustrations from which it stems nonetheless open the way to reckless elements among black, as well as white, student militants.

The universities must now choose among three courses: a principled but flexible response to legitimate black demands; a dogmatic, repressive adherence to traditional, liberal, and essentially racist policies; and a cowardly surrender to all black demands, no matter how destructive to the university as an institution of higher learning or to American and Afro-American society in general. This last option, which has been taken in a notable number of places, ironically reflects as much racism in its assumptions and implications as the second, and it takes little skill in prophecy to realize that its conclusion will be a bloodbath in which blacks are once again the chief victims. Yet, the debate over black studies proceeds without attention to the major features of the alternatives; it proceeds, in fact, in a manner that suggests the very paternalistic white racism against which so many blacks are today protesting.

The demand for black studies and for special black studies departments needs no elaborate explanation or defense. It rests on an awareness of the unique and dual nature of the black experience in the United States. Unlike European immigrants, blacks came here involuntarily, were enslaved and excluded from access to the mainstream of American life, and as a result have had a special history with a profoundly national-cultural dimension. Unlike, say, Italo-Americans, Afro-Americans have within their history the elements of a

distinct nationality at the same time that they have participated in and contributed immensely to a common American
nationality. Despite the efforts of many black and some white
scholars, this paradoxical experience has yet to be explored
with the respect and intellectual rigor it deserves.

This essential justification for black studies, incidentally,
raises serious questions about the demands by white radicals
for "ethnic studies" and for special attention to people from
the "third world," especially since the term "third world" is,
from a Marxist and revolutionary point of view, a reactionary
swindle. These demands, when sincere, have their origin in a
proper concern for the fate of Mexican-Americans, Puerto
Ricans, Asians, and other ethnic groups in a white-racist
culture, but the study of the attendant problems does not, at
least on the face of it, require anything like an approach
similar to that of black studies. For the most part, the discrimination against these groups is largely a class question,
requiring sober analysis of class structure in America; for the
rest, much of the racism directed against these minorities can
be traced directly to the by-products of the enslavement of
blacks by whites and the ideology derived therefrom. In any
case, the issues are clearly different, for the black question is
simultaneously one of class and nationality (not merely
minority ethnic status), and it is therefore a disservice to the
cause of black liberation to construct a politically opportunist
equation that can only blur the unique and central quality of
the black experience in the United States.

The duality of the black experience haunts the present debate and leads us immediately into a consideration of the ideological and political features of the black studies programs.
It is, at best, irrelevant to argue, as DeVere E. Pentony does
in the April, 1969, issue of the *Atlantic,* that all professors of
history and social science bring a particular ideology and

politics to their classroom and that a black ideological bias is no worse than any other. There is no such thing as a black ideology or a black point of view. Rather there are various black-nationalist biases, from left-wing versions such as that of the Panthers to right-wing versions such as that of Ron Karenga and other "cultural nationalists." There are also authentic sections of the black community that retain conservative, liberal, or radical integrationist and antinationalist positions. Both integrationist and separatist tendencies can be militant or moderate, radical or conservative (in the sense generally applied to white politics in relation to social questions). The separatists are riding high today, and the integrationists are beating a retreat; but this has happened before and may be reversed tomorrow.

All these elements have a right to participate in the exploration of black historical and cultural themes. In one sense, the whole point of black studies programs in a liberal arts college or university ought to be to provide for the widest and most vigorous exchange among all these groups in an atmosphere of free discussion and mutual toleration. The demand for an exclusively black faculty and especially the reactionary demand for student control of autonomous departments must be understood as demands for the introduction of specific ideological and political criteria into the selection of faculty and the composition of programs. Far from being proposals to relate these programs to the black community, they are in fact factionally based proposals to relate them to one or another political tendency within the black community and to exclude others. The bloody, but by no means isolated, feud between black student factions on the UCLA campus ought to make that clear.

One of the new hallmarks of white racism is the notion of one black voice, one black experience, one black political community, one black ideology—of a black community without an authentic inner political life wracked by discussion and ideological struggle. In plain truth, what appears on the campuses as "what the blacks want" is almost invariably what the dominant faction in a particular black caucus wants. Like all people who fight for liberation, blacks are learning the value of organizational discipline and subordination to a firm and united line of action. Sometimes, the formulation of particular demands and actions has much less to do with their intrinsic merits or with the institution under fire than with the momentary balance in the struggle for power within the caucus itself. This discipline presents nothing unprincipled or sinister, but it does present difficult and painful problems, which must be evaluated independently by those charged with institutional and political responsibility in the white community.

The pseudo-revolutionary middle-class totalitarians who constitute one temporarily powerful wing of the left-wing student movement understand this dimension, even if few others seem to. Accordingly, they support demands for student control as an entering wedge for a general political purge of faculties, a purge they naïvely hope to dominate. These suburban putschists are most unlikely to succeed in their stated objectives of purging "reactionaries," for they are isolated, incoherent, and without adequate power. But they may very well help to reestablish the principle of the campus purge and thereby provide a moral and legal basis for a new wave of McCarthyism. The disgraceful treatment of Professors Staughton Lynd and Jesse Lemisch, among many who have been recently purged from universities by both liberal and right-wing pressure, has already set a tone of renewed repression, which some fanatical and unreasoning left-wing militants are unwittingly reinforcing. If black studies departments are permitted to become political bases and cadre-training schools for one or another political movement, the door will be open for the conversion of other departments to similar roles; that door is already being forced in some places.

Those blacks who speak in harsh nationalist accents in favor of all-black faculties, departmental autonomy, and student power open themselves to grave suspicions of bad faith. The most obvious objection, raised sharply by several outstanding black educators in the South, concerns the systematic raiding of black colleges by financially stronger white ones. The shortage of competent black specialists in black history, social science, and black culture is a matter of general knowledge and concern. Hence, the successful application of the all-black principle in most universities would spell the end of hopes to build one or more distinguished black universities to serve as a center for the training of a national Afro-American intelligentsia. One need not be partial to black nationalism in any of its varieties to respect the right of black people to self-determination, for this right flows directly from the duality of their unique experience in the United States. Even those who dislike or distrust black nationalism as such should be able to view the development of such centers of higher education as positive and healthy. If there is no place in the general American university for ideological homogeneity and conformity, there is a place in American society for universities based on adherence to a specific ideology, as the Catholic universities, for example, have demonstrated.

Responsible black scholars have been working hard for an end to raiding and to the scattering of the small number of black professors across the country. Among other obstacles, they face the effort of ostensibly nationalist black students who seek to justify their decision to attend predominantly white institutions, often of high prestige, by fighting for a larger black teaching staff. The outcome of these demands is the obscurantist nonsense that black studies can and should be taught by people without intellectual credentials since these credentials are "white" anyway. It is true that many black men are capable of teaching important college-level courses even though they do not have formal credentials. For example, the Afro-American tradition in music, embracing slave songs, spirituals, blues, jazz, and other forms, could probably be taught best by a considerable number of articulate and cultured, if sometimes self-taught, black musicians and free-lance critics who are largely unknown to the white community. But few good universities have ever refused to waive formalities in any field when genuine intellectual credentials of a nonacademic order could be provided. What has to be resisted firmly is the insanity that claims, as in one recent instance, that experience as a SNCC field organizer should be considered more important than a Ph.D. in the hiring of a professor of Afro-American history. This assertion represents a general contempt for all learning and a particular contempt for black studies as a field of study requiring disciplined, serious intellectual effort—an attitude that reflects the influence of white racism, even when brought forth by a black man.

The demand for all-black faculties rests on the insistence that only blacks can understand the black experience. This cant is nothing new: it forms the latest version of the battle cry of every reactionary nationalism and has clear antecedents, for example, in the nineteenth-century German Romantic movement. To be perfectly blunt, it now constitutes an ideologically fascist position and must be understood as such. The general reply to it—if one is necessary—is simply that the history of every people can only be written from within and without. But there is a specific reply too. However much the black presence has produced a unique and distinctly national Afro-American experience, it has also formed part of a broader, integrated national culture. It would be absurd to try to understand the history of, say, the South without carefully studying black history. Any Southern historian worth his salt must also be a historian of black America—and vice versa —and if so, it would be criminal to deny him an opportunity to teach his proper subject. Certainly, these remarks do not add up to an objection to a preference for black departmental directors and a numerical predominance of blacks on the faculty, if possible, for every people must write its own history and play the main role in the formation of its own intelligentsia and national culture. These measures would be justified simply on grounds of the need to establish relations of confidence with black students, for they involve no sacrifice of principle and do not compromise the integrity of the university. But preference and emphasis are one thing; monopoly and ideological exclusion are quite another.

We might mention here the problem of the alleged "psychological need" of black people to do this or that or to be this or that in order to reclaim their manhood, reestablish their ostensibly lost dignity, and God knows what else. There is a place for these questions in certain kinds of intellectual discussions and in certain political forums, but there is no place for these questions in the formation of university policy. In such a context they represent a benevolent paternalism that is neither more nor less than racist. Whites in general and university professors and administrators in particular are not required to show "sympathy," "compassion," "understanding," and other manifestations of liberal guilt feelings; they are required to take black demands seriously—to take them straight, on their merits. That is, they are required to treat political demands politically and to meet their responsibility to fight white racism while also meeting their responsibility to defend the integrity and dignity of the university community as a whole.

Only if the universities have a clear attitude toward themselves will they be able to fulfill their duty to the black community. Our universities, if they are to survive—and their survival is problematical—must redefine themselves as institutions of higher learning and firmly reject the role of cadre-training schools for government, business, or community organizations of any kind. Blame for the present crisis ought to be placed on those who, especially after World War II, opened the universities to the military, to big-business recruitment, to the "fight against Communism," to the CIA, and to numerous other rightist pressures. If Dow Chemical or ROTC belongs on a college campus, so does the Communist Party, the Black Panthers, the John Birch Society, the Campfire Girls, or the Mafia for that matter. Students have a clear political right to organize on campuses as Democrats, Republicans, Communists, Panthers, or whatever, provided their activities are appropriate to campus life, but the universities have no business making special institutional arrangements with this or that faction off campus and then putting down other factions as illicit. And government and business represent political intrusions quite as much as do political parties. The same is true for the anachronistic and absurd practice of having American universities controlled by boards of trustees instead of by their faculties in consultation with the students. In short, the black studies question, like the black revolt as a whole, has raised all the fundamental problems of class power in American life, and the solutions will have to run deep into the structure of the institutions themselves.

What the universities owe to black America is what they owe to white America: an atmosphere of freedom and dissent for the pursuit of higher learning. Black people have largely been excluded in the past, for the atmosphere has been racist, the history and culture of black people have been ignored or caricatured, and access to the universities themselves has been severely circumscribed. Black studies programs, shaped in a manner consistent with such traditional university values as ideological freedom and diversity, can help to correct this injustice. So can scholarships and financial assistance to black students and special facilities for those blacks who wish to live and work with some degree of ethnic homogeneity. But no university is required to surrender its basic standards of competence in the selection of faculty or the admission of students. If not enough black students are equipped to enter college today, it is because of atrocious conditions in lower education. The universities can take a few steps to correct this injustice, but the real fight must take place elsewhere in society and must be aimed at providing black communities with the financial resources, independence, and autonomy necessary to educate their people properly from the earliest appropriate ages. There are limits to what a particular institution like a university can do, and it dare not try to solve problems that can be solved only by the political institutions of society as a whole. And above all, no university need surrender its historical role and essential content in order to right the wrongs of the whole political and social system; it need only reform itself to contribute to a solution of the broader problems in a manner consistent with its character as a place of higher learning with limited functions, possibilities, and responsibilities.

Black studies programs have two legitimate tasks. First, they can, by their very nature, provide a setting within which black people can forge an intelligentsia equipped to provide leadership on various levels of political and cultural action. Black studies programs themselves can do only part of this job. For that reason many able and sophisticated sections of the Black Student Alliance organizations wisely call on their brothers and sisters to participate in these programs but also to specialize in medicine, engineering, sociology, economic analysis, or in fact any scientific or humanistic field. They know that only the emergence of a fully developed intelligentsia, with training in every field of knowledge, can ultimately meet the deepest needs of the black community. In this respect, notwithstanding strong elements of nihilism in their own organizations, their seriousness, maturity, discipline, and realism stand in striking contrast to the childish anti-intellectualism of those bourgeois whites who currently claim to speak for the radical student movement and who impose upon it their own version of generational revolt.

Second, black studies can help immeasurably to combat the racism of white students. The exclusion of whites from the faculty and student body of the black studies programs would therefore defeat half the purpose of the programs themselves. Undoubtedly, there are problems. To the extent that black students view these courses as places of refuge where they can rap with their brothers, they are certain to resent the white presence, not to mention a possible white numerical predominance among the student body. Black students who want an exclusively black setting are entitled to it—in a black university. They are not entitled to tear any institution apart to suit their present mood. The universities owe black people a chance to get a liberal or technical education, but that debt can only be paid in a way consistent with the proper role of the university in society. Beyond that, no university may safely go. If it tries, the result can only be the end of any worthwhile higher education. The inability of so many radical whites to grasp this obvious point is especially galling. It ought to be obvious that the elite schools will protect themselves from this kind of degradation, even if they continue to accept the degradation that accompanies complicity with the war machine and with big business. It is the others—the ones serving the working-class and lower-middle-class youth—that will perish or be transformed into extensions of low-grade high schools. Universities must resist the onslaught now being made against them by superficially radical bourgeois students who have exploited the struggles over black studies programs to advance their own tactical objectives. Fortunately, these elements do not speak for the radical student movement as a whole but represent only a tendency within it; the internal diversity of organizations like SDS, for example, far exceeds the level revealed in the press.

No matter how painful some of the battles are or will become, the advent of black studies programs represents a momentous step toward the establishment of relations of equality between white and black intellectuals. But, if these programs are to realize their potential in support of black liberation and in the fostering of genuinely free and critical scholarship, our universities must resolve honestly the questions of limits and legitimacy. Those who blindly ignore or cynically manipulate these questions, and the reforms they imply, corrupt the meaning of black studies and risk the destruction of institutions necessary to the preservation of freedom in American life.

A Charade of Power: Black Students at White Colleges

BY KENNETH B. CLARK

*Kenneth B. Clark, a social psychologist, was born in Panama and re-
ceived his A.B. from Howard University and Ph.D. from Columbia
University. He has taught at Hampton Institute and the City College
of New York. He has also been Director of New York's Northside
Center for Child Development and President of the Metropolitan
Applied Research Center, Incorporated. Members of the Supreme
Court read his works on the impact of segregation on Negro children
before the Court's school desegregation decision in 1954. Clark's books
include* Negro Protest, Negro Students at Integrated Colleges, Prejudice and Your Child, A Relevant War Against Poverty, *and* Dark
Ghetto. *When Antioch College established a separate Black Studies
program open only to black students, Clark resigned from Antioch's
Board of Directors. In his letter of resignation, Clark charged that
Antioch had adopted the position of segregationists by its "primitive
exclusion" of white students from the program and was participating
in "a shoddy evasion of the moral and educational responsibility" of an
educational institution. Believing that prejudice and discrimination "are
damaging to the human personality," Clark asserted that "racial distinctions are arbitrary, dangerously ignorant, and cruel. They are
destructive and inimical to all of the goals of serious education." Con-
cluding his letter of resignation, Clark charged: "In permitting a group
of students to inflict their dogmatism and ideology on other students
and on the total college community; and in being silent while some
students intimidate, threaten, and in some cases physically assault the
Negro students who disagree with them, the Administration at Antioch
has not only defaulted in its responsibilities, but, I believe has made a
mockery of its concern for the protection and development of human
dignity without regard to cost." Clark later expanded his views on
Black Studies in the following essay which appeared in the* Antioch

Reprinted by permission from *The Antioch Review* XXIX, no. 2 (Summer,
1969): 145–48.

Review. Contending that black students have only succumbed to a new form of racism in establishing separate Black Studies programs, Clark argues that the victories they have won give them the semblance but not the substance of power.

THE DILEMMA of the Negro, especially of the black college student, in these turbulent days is full of irony and paradox. His dilemma is compounded by the appearance of change in American institutions, particularly education, and his need to respond appropriately in terms of the degree of reality of this change. He often finds that change is an illusion, that he is presented with, and seems sometimes to invite, merely new forms of racism, in new guises but, in the end, made of the same stuff.

His dilemma is rooted in one dominant fact: however noisy his rhetoric, however flamboyant the manifestations of his protest, he is still the minority. Even his "victories" are guided and permitted by the majority. The armed black students at Cornell had no real power—not they, but the white majority were in control. The fact that the white administration and faculty chose not to act violently in response, but rather to acquiesce—or appear to acquiesce—to demands, did not obscure the evidence of real power. The guns at the ready were a charade; they were permitted only because the majority understood they could be put down whenever it wished to do so. To the extent that whites encourage in blacks acceptance of this pretense of power, they are participating in but one more manifestation of an old racism.

Negroes have had centuries of experience of benevolent racism that permits bizarre behavior on the grounds that the Negro is going through a phase that will be outgrown. Whites believe this now—and often state it candidly. Black separatism, particularly among the young, is seen as racially adolescent behavior, to be understood, tolerated, and even condoned as long as it does not threaten the real sources of authority. That many black students do not grasp the pervasive and subtle forms of white racism is clear in their exultant reaction after "non-negotiable" demands lead to apparent concessions. They believe that Black Studies Institutes, separate from the governance of the university, free from the regulations of faculty or degree requirements, or black dormitories from which whites are "excluded," are evidence of surrender of majority power. But whites have not given up, thereby, anything other than the requirement of persistent confrontation with blacks on a basis of black equality. Negro students miss the fact that voluntary surrender of "power" by those who hold it is seldom loss of actual power. Symbolic power may be tendered, however, particularly when those in authority perceive that negotiators will be satisfied with the mere appearance of power, indeed, that in some complex way, they may prefer not to take the risk of competing for the responsibility of genuine power. Those in power seldom give up more than is necessary to restore stability—for stability is essential to their orderly exercise of authority.

If a mayor can buy peace by strategic patronage (no less patronage when black militants rather than old-fashioned ward-healers demand it), he will do so. He need not transform the ghetto into a viable community if this is not the non-negotiable demand. If a white-dominated Board of Education can appease militants, and simultaneously strengthen top quality white-segregated schools, it need not insist on basic reorganization of the system. If a national political leader can ease the pressure by offers of subsidies to a few black capitalists, he need not move to abolish poverty, among both Negroes and whites. If a university administration can restore harmony and the image of innovation by a no-strings-attached financial grant to a separate black studies program that may cover a few salaries or subsidize a gas station, it need not move to transform itself into a genuinely nonracial institution dedicated to developing human beings and to helping them develop effective strategies for fundamental social change. No more power is granted than it is necessary to yield.

A Tempting Choice

It is probably true that many black students understand this and, in cynicism born from despair at the tenacious hold of white racism, take what can be easily won, settling for the charade. It is, in many ways, a tempting choice. Many probably know, though the admission is too painful to endure, that a university could not surrender to student control a Black Studies Institute with exclusionary characteristics and without even minimal academic standards if it truly valued the humanity of blacks. If the university does not insist that Negroes be as rigorously trained as whites to compete in the arena of real power, or that studies of racism be as thoroughly and systematically pursued as studies of nuclear physics, one must question whether it is really serious.

It is clear that whites desperately need to know the history, the psychology, the economics of their own racism, yet a university that agrees promptly and without struggle to exclude whites from such studies, except in isolation from militant blacks, has in fact protected whites from ruthless encounter with that knowledge. Painful though such confrontation would be, whites need to face with a terrible honesty the consequences of their own inheritance, and they need to do it in the presence of blacks. One can surely understand their reluctance to do so, for, although Negroes cannot escape the daily encounter with themselves as Negroes, whites can and usually do seem to escape the necessity of facing themselves as whites. They are not consciously aware of race every moment of every day, as Negroes are. They are able to train themselves as economists, as lawyers, without such concerns; they are able to live as human beings without conscious modification. Why—if they are rational, non-masochist individuals—should they present themselves to be flagellated or, even more painful, commit themselves to a genuine struggle for equality if it is not required? Why, particularly, if blacks collaborate in helping them by rewarding such evasion of reality with accolades of radical relevance? If the white applauds black separatism and at the same time enhances his liberal image, he has the best of both worlds—he need not challenge white domination of all institutions in America, and he is absolved from guilt all at once.

One must understand and respond to the reluctance of blacks to further the education of whites, especially at deep emotional cost. However, it is more difficult to accept the collusion of many of the most creative and brilliant of young black leaders in programs that are separate and unequal. Must the struggle against racism be given up so easily? Has a realistic despair been rationalized by a decision that competition for genuine power to achieve positive social change is itself undesirable—not only that it is unachievable, but also that it is undesirable, corrupt evidence of a corrupt society? It may indeed be true that it is hopeless to try to change the deeply rooted racism in American society. Certainly, those confined to Nazi concentration camps would have been right in an appraisal of their own situation as hopeless. But is it required of blacks that they, as some concentration camp inmates did— according to Viktor Frankl and Bruno Bettelheim—identify with the oppressor, collaborate in the efficient implementation of his goals, and rationalize this surrender of spirit and integrity as a realistic adaptation?

The New Black Monasteries

It may well be that stubborn commitment to an integrated—an equal—society is unrealistic, and that an unremitting search for strategies to achieve it, therefore, is irrational, given the forces arrayed against it. Those who predicted "the wave of the future" in the face of the apparently irresistible Nazi onrush certainly would have agreed. But history is littered with the ruins of unconquerable empires and irresistible crusades. And, even if the predictions of defeat are correct, would a retreat into the new black monasteries with their secret rituals and their new theologies be the rational (or even the most comforting) solution? How long can one accept exclusion as a self-desiratum? When one leaves college to enter the outside world one can either create new enclaves, a ghetto within the ghetto, or can struggle to free the ghetto's inhabitants.

And if one enters the hard struggle for freedom, one must bring resources and skills to the inevitable encounter with the majority, who have built and guarded the ghetto's walls and fostered and profited from its ruin. Even if one could retreat oneself, can young blacks face the desperate need of their brothers—without response? The ghetto resident has not chosen his exclusion; it is forced upon him. There are no rats in the black dormitories. They are an unreal haven. Life within them, while warm, and deeply comforting, and intensely exhilarating—like the womb, cannot sustain life long. White segregationists could devise no better strategy than to persuade white liberals that they could absolve themselves from corrosive guilt by supporting black exclusion (under less rigorous standards than those required for white exclusion) in the heart of that institution most likely to provide black leaders for the future—the university—and at the same time, to persuade many of the best young black students that this is a radical victory.

But no such strategy needs to be devised, for the symbiotic needs of each group help to sustain it: the need of the guilty white to feel innocent again, the need of the angry young black to nurse his pain in private. Together they serve the cause of inequality. The ultimate victory of white racism would be to encourage black suicide—whether the suicide of physical self-destruction or the suicide of self-imposed withdrawal from the conditions of life.

This is the contemporary dilemma of the Negro in American universities. Whether the dilemma will be resolved in time to save the nation from the consequences of its history is still unclear. But even if despair is the only realism, there remain fundamental values and ideals by which one must live, even in despair. One cannot make the life of racism palatable.

Black Studies at Antioch

BY STEPHEN LYTHCOTT

Stephen Lythcott, a black student at Antioch, answered the charges leveled at the Antioch Black Studies program by Kenneth Clark. He accuses people such as Clark of being so conditioned by the emotional struggle for desegregation of the last few decades that they are incapable of seeing alternatives to segregation or integration. Lythcott argues that blacks face too many pressing problems to be concerned with what Clark saw as the central problem of our society: the need to eradicate the white man's ignorance of blacks. The Antioch program, oriented toward social action, concrete problems, and uplifting the black community, Lythcott contends, is a realistic approach to a racist America and is free from the repressive forces which an open-door policy for students and faculty would encourage.

WITHIN THE PAST YEAR or two Black Studies programs have been established at all kinds of colleges across the entire United States. Despite the growth and popularity of this aspect of the Black liberation movement, few people seem to understand what Black Studies programs are really about.

Most socially concerned Americans have vivid memories of the "civil rights movement," the days of sit-ins, freedom rides and other demonstrations for an integrated society. I was fortunate to have been involved in the first sit-in demonstration of the "modern" period, which occurred in Oklahoma City in 1958, and which was carried out before the NAACP actually sanctioned such activity. I remember the men who blocked the doors at restaurants, and physically removed us

Reprinted by permission from *The Antioch Review* XXIX, no. 2 (Summer, 1969): 149–54.

from hotel lobbies. I was only eight years old at that time, and had participated in the company of my older sister, but I remember very well.

I also remember yelling "Free by '63" at NAACP conventions, but when 1963 came around we were not free. And we still are not free.

Getting our freedom by 1963 only meant that by that time the government would pass a law allowing Black people to go anywhere they wanted. That kind of freedom could be achieved by law. It could be granted by a proclamation, much like Lincoln's a century ago. What kind of freedom did that give us?

Freedom, as I see it, means the freedom to develop and grow. Since the beginning of history, progress and development in the western world have been perceived subjectively and exclusively by those who have gained from it. Development has been a one-sided concept. The tiny countries of Belgium and the Netherlands prospered the more that they subjected and exploited their vast colonies, the Congo and Indonesia. The same relationship obtains between every colonial master and its colony.

America has been able to develop into a dominant world power largely as a result of the toil and servitude of slaves on Southern plantations and the cheap labor of colonized Blacks in Northern factories and industrial fields. Never in history has any colonial people been allowed to develop independently of their overlords.

It is this freedom to create an independent economic and social foundation in the community that is the essence of the situation. The question of integration or separation is but an illusory incantation.

Those who participated in the civil rights movement, the "crusade" for integration, were distinguished by varying degrees of commitment to and involvement with the goal of Black liberation. The most regrettable consequence of this protest movement is that Black people, during the nineteen-fifties and sixties, were effectively conditioned to think in terms of a dualism. Their responses were polarized between two concepts: Segregation and/or Integration. Most Black people, and whites too, came to be incapable of conceiving alternatives to this situation. The Antioch Afro-American Studies Institute does not intend to become entrapped by this kind of polarized mentality.

The Institute and Dr. Clark

It is a pity that many Black people remain victims of this kind of mental conditioning, especially people as presumably enlightened as Dr. Kenneth Clark, who recently resigned from the Antioch College Board of Trustees over the issue of the Afro-American Studies Institute. It is unfortunate, if perhaps unsurprising, that in the year 1969 a man of Dr. Clark's stature would be so distracted by implications of separatism in the Black community that he would apply the values of 1954 to the development of that community. It is equally unfortunate that Dr. Clark is so blinded by the refractions of movement within the Black student community that he loses all sight of prudence and judicial wisdom.

Antioch administrators, AASI students, fellow trustees, and alumni of the College have all asked Dr. Clark to come to the campus in order to reach a fair appraisal of what is actually happening in Yellow Springs. He has declined these invitations. (For that matter Dr. Clark attended only two meetings of the Board of Trustees during his entire tenure as a member.) He has attacked the AASI without asking us for the facts of our presence. He has disparaged the courses offered by AASI as inferior to the general college curriculum, but he has consulted no one who has taken those courses, has made no inquiry into our curriculum. He has condemned the Institute for racial exclusion without offering the factual evidence to support his charges, and without discernibly stirring himself to seek that evidence. Thus Dr. Clark has done a disservice to himself and to the entire Black community by relying on hearsay testimony and second-hand opinion as the source of his criticism of the Afro-American Studies Institute.

Members of the AASI retain respect for Dr. Clark as a scholar. His book *Dark Ghetto* is still required reading for all students in the AASI program.

White Need, Black Responsibility

It is often argued that white people need to learn about Black people more than do Black people themselves. Although I could not endorse this formulation of the problem, I will say that white people have a vast ignorance of the Black man and his history and burdens in America. However, the fact remains that the major task of reorienting the Black college student, creating a new value system for him, and additionally putting his knowledge and skills at the disposal of the people he has forgotten in the Black community—these claims have the highest priority for us, are far more pertinent to our situation.

AASI does not presume to have either the time or the resources to meet the cultural needs, minister to the residual guilt, or deal with the subtle inbred racism of hundreds of white students within the Antioch community. Neither does it wish to participate in the paternalistic white effort to redeem the ghettos of this country with generous infusions of suburban values.

I'll never forget the situation of an interracial class in African History which I once attended. The professor was trying to explain to us the significance of Egypt's great influence on the rest of civilization. He had to spend a number of hours making a majority of the white students understand that Cleopatra and the rest of ancient Egypt was a part of Black history, just as much a part as the ancient kingdom of Ghana, or the African slave trade. Indeed, Black students have their hands full already, without assuming the extra burdens of white education!

Through a Lens, Darkly

From the very beginning the American press has distorted and damaged the movement to create Black Studies programs. We are not surprised by this, since the press distorts most of the controversial topics it deals with. The mass media has sought to disseminate and sensationalize its own version of student activism, an activism characterized by revolutionary zeal and fiery-eyed rhetoric. From all of this, the stereotype Black Militant has arisen: a dashiki-clad student ranting about white racism and the irrelevancy of the white curriculum. His demands for Black Studies programs are made to appear as spontaneous, irrational attempts to get a few "soul courses" with which to somehow liberate himself. Most people now seem to think that AASI and other Black Studies programs are merely aggrandized bull-sessions about "negritude," or a residential opportunity for collective navel-gazing and the consumption of chitterlings. Black Studies institutes cannot be so easily dismissed.

Black students are not so naive that we think we can dance

our way to freedom. One has but to look at the components of the AASI curriculum to realize this. The AASI curriculum is founded on social need and is aimed at social action. In Spring, '69 AASI offered 22 courses, most of them in the Humanities and Social Sciences. At present we are not qualified to teach the Physical Sciences. Students interested in the physical sciences and related fields still take courses in the general Antioch curriculum, along with their AASI classes.

Since in the past we have been a fairly small group (approximately 100 students spread over Antioch's two divisions), we have not had the money to employ full-time faculty; nor have we wanted to contribute to the "brain drain" of Black educators from predominantly Black colleges. Instead, we have engaged qualified "consultants" to teach some of our courses. They teach a course called "Survival (In a Crisis Situation)" as well as courses in economics, history, sociology, and psychology. In addition, AASI sponsors classes in the creative arts, such as music, drama, dance, and language, and courses in Islamic studies, which are taught by interested and qualified students.

Our consultants are all Black Ph.D. candidates at the University of Chicago. They visit the campus once a month for three days of classes. During this period they lecture for ten hours a day. The consultants help evaluate Antioch's curriculum to determine what courses should be taken along with their lectures. (For example, and obviously, 18th to 20th century European history—to reveal the origins and nature of European colonialism.) All the lectures are recorded and put in a tape library. Between the visits of the consultants the tapes are used for reference and as the basis of class discussions. During these times the classes are led by student assistants who are being trained to eventually assume the role and the responsibility of the consultants. We expect this form of consultant teaching to spread to a number of other Black Studies programs.

The Institute's courses are different from those in the regular Antioch curriculum. (If anything is "regular" at Antioch.) We do not concern ourselves with every major figure in an academic discipline, nor do we labor over abstractions or over theories of general or liberal education. Our economics courses, for example, are designed to deal with concrete as well as theoretical economic problems within the Black community, and to produce solutions to them. Likewise our psychology courses deal with vital problems of the Black man and his psychic attitudes; these are the problems and attitudes that will limit his future and inhibit his development in this country. We deal with concrete schisms and prejudices within ourselves. For a white student to be in any of these sessions would only blunt the knife, and inhibit fundamental emotions from being expressed. It would be very detrimental to the entire program.

Town and Gown

As a communiversity, AASI transfers knowledge gained from the campus program to the Black community, and in turn it brings experience gained in the community back to the Institute. Although we are still based on the Antioch campus in Yellow Springs, plans are well under way for our relocation to West Dayton, a distance of some 30 miles. We are remodeling a building in the Black community there which will house our offices and classrooms. Houses are being negotiated for living quarters. This move will allow the Institute to carry out its activities far more realistically and effectively. It will be a field department of the college. However, spending our first year on the Antioch campus has been a very fruitful experience for AASI students. Therefore, in order to develop certain skills and a sense of communal living and unity, AASI freshmen will continue to spend a preparatory period on campus before they join the "field center."

AASI is operating a gas station and garage in Cincinnati. Though such a franchise tends not to be very profitable on a short-term basis, we have been able to supply jobs to a lot of people in the Black community there, and thus to create an opportunity for them to develop vocational skills. The Institute has also opened a bookstore in Springfield. The store is run as a cooperative, and is presently operated by a coalition of Black students from colleges in this area, along with members of the Black community in Springfield. Our hope is that this program will serve as a nucleus for cooperative economic, social and political action, leading toward the unification of the Black Springfield community.

Some local observers have concluded that the Institute's ventures into commerce reveal an acceptance of the values of "Black capitalism," an alleged solution to the Black man's plight which has been advanced by President Nixon, among other committed public servants. It would be folly for anyone to think that Black Capitalism is the answer to the Black man's economic condition in this country. The word "black" does not change the nature of capitalism, does not alter the roles of the exploiter and the exploited. Indeed, there are Black people in this country who are not above exploiting their own people. The members of AASI do not intend to encourage such entrepreneurs. The answer to us seems to lie in a cooperative economy. Black people should think in terms of communal organizations and joint ownerships of commercial enterprises, and this can complement their political thinking in terms of social unity and united organizational action.

The Marketplace of Free Ideas

It seems that the main criticisms brought against Black Studies programs are that some of them practice exclusionary policies and some of them deny freedom of inquiry to the general scholarly community. The idea of freedom of inquiry is, I suppose, a noble one. Many scholars say that it has constituted the cornerstone of most respected institutions of higher learning. Unfortunately, civilization in this country has evolved to the point where man cannot always trust his fellow man; even more unfortunately this climate of mistrust has now settled over the academic community.

Antioch College itself has discovered to its disillusionment that this condition of mistrust is an immediate reality. After several incidents of attempted (and successful) rapes, thefts, and fights, the College has had to revise its notion of an open community. It has had to tighten its regulations so as to stop the flow of outsiders or "undesirables" into the campus.

It is gratifying that AASI, at its inception, was able to foresee the dangers of attempting to maintain a free, open-door community. Most Antiochians believe it to be a matter of fact that government agents are at work on the campus, for one reason or another. In view of the Federal government's increasingly repressive actions against most anti-establishment organizations, and in view of its commitment to maintaining a capitalist, war-supported economy and a colonialist society, no Black Studies program like the AASI could exist with an open-door policy for very long before being infiltrated and undermined by these repressive forces.

What should universities do? Should they confront the present reality realistically, or should they ignore and explain away troublesome problems? If we are going to ignore such immediate and undeniable problems as those I have indicated, just to pay homage to the concept of freedom of inquiry, then we are going to isolate ourselves in our ivory towers of intellectualism even further. We will continue to restrict our concerns to those of utopian communities like Yellow Springs, Ohio. We will forget what lies beyond these sylvan pastures and seemingly tranquil halls.

What worse crime could there be?

The Road to the Top is Through Higher Education –Not Black Studies

BY W. ARTHUR LEWIS

William Arthur Lewis, professor of economics and international affairs at Princeton University, was born in the West Indies and educated at the University of London. He has taught at Williams, Toronto, Wales, and Manchester University, and served as vice-chancellor of the University of the West Indies. Professor Lewis has also served as adviser to several West African countries and conducted research on the cost of education. The best known of his several books is The Theory of Economic Growth. *Professor Lewis rejects the idea that black students should concentrate on Black Studies and calls instead for them to study those subjects which will enable them to obtain an equitable share of the top- and middle-level jobs in the American economy. While Nathan Hare and June Jordan argue that black students are searching for a new vision of themselves and ways to improve the black community in Black Studies, Lewis contends that separate community development is an idle dream unless blacks can go outside the community to earn money in the same way that other ethnic groups do. In order to do this they must study the same subjects that other students who become presidents and managers of American corporations study.*

W HEN A FRIEND SUGGESTED that, since I had spent all my adult life in black-power movements and in universities, I might make some comments on the highly topical subject of black power in the American university, it did not at first seem to be a good idea. Now that I have come to grips with it I am

Reprinted by permission from *The New York Times Magazine*, May 11, 1969.

even more conscious of my folly in tackling so difficult and controversial a subject.

I am also very conscious that my credentials are inadequate, since the black-power movements in the countries with which I am familiar differ fundamentally from black power in the United States. My stamping grounds are the West Indies, where I was born, and Africa, where I have worked, and which I shall be visiting for the fourteenth time next month. But in both those places blacks are the great majority of the people—97 per cent in Jamaica, 99 per cent in Nigeria. The objective of the political movements was therefore to capture the central legislature, and the executive and judicial powers. In the United States, in contrast, blacks are only 11 per cent of the population, and have neither claim to nor prospect of capturing the Congress, the executive branch, or the Supreme Court for themselves alone. The objectives have to be different, and the strategy must also be different. Comparison between the colonial situation and the position of blacks in America is bound to mislead if it is suggested as a basis for deciding political strategy.

The fact of the matter is that the struggle of the blacks in America is a unique experience, with no parallel in Africa. And since it is unique, the appropriate strategies are likely to be forged only by trial and error. We are all finding the process a great trial, and since our leaders are going off in all directions at once, a great deal of error is also inevitable. I myself, in venturing onto this ground, claim the protection of the First Amendment, but do not aspire to wear the cloak of Papal infallibility.

The goals and tactics of black power in America have to be adjusted to the reality of America. Take the issue of segregation. Everywhere in the black world, except among a small minority of American blacks, the fight against segregation has been in the foreground of black-power movements. This goes without saying in countries where blacks are the great majority; yet there are situations where a minority may strengthen itself by temporary self-segregation of a limited kind.

All American minorities have passed through a stage of temporary self-segregation, not just the Afro-Americans. Foreigners speak of the United States as a "melting pot" and it may one day be that; but for the present America is really not a melting pot but a welding shop. It is a country in which many different groups of people live and work together side by side, without coalescing. There are Poles, and Irish, and Chinese, and Jews, and Germans, and many other ethnic groups.

But their way of living together is set by the clock; there is integration between 7 o'clock in the morning and 5 o'clock at night, when all mingle and work together in the center of the city, in the banks and factories, department stores and universities. But after 5 o'clock each ethnic group returns to its own neighborhood. There it has its own separate social life. There Poles do not marry Italians, even though they are both white Catholics. The neighborhood has its own schools, its own little shops, its own doctors, and its own celebrations. Integration by day is accompanied by segregation by night.

It is important to note that this self-segregation is voluntary and not imposed by law. An Italian *can* buy a house in an Irish neighborhood if he wishes to do so, *can* marry an Irish girl, and *can* go to an Irish Catholic Church. Many people also insist that this voluntary segregation is only a temporary phase in the acculturation of ethnic groups. They live together until they have found their feet on the American way of life, after which they disperse. The immigrants from Germany and Scandinavia have for the most part already moved out of segregated neighborhoods. The Irish and the Jews are just in the process, and sooner or later the Poles, the Chinese and even the Afro-Americans may disperse. But in the meantime this voluntary self-segregation shelters those who are not yet ready to lose themselves completely in the American mainstream. Other people believe that there will always be cultural pluralism in America, and that this may even be a source of strength. Whether or not they are right about the long run, there is no disputing that voluntary social self-segregation is the current norm.

The black-power movement is therefore fully in the American tradition in recognizing that certain neighborhoods are essentially black neighborhoods, where the black politician, the black doctor, the black teacher, the black grocer and the black clergyman are going to be able to play roles which are not open to them, *de facto,* in other neighborhoods. Many Southern Negroes claim vigorously that blacks are better off in the South than in the North precisely because the Southern white philosophy has reserved a place for a black middle class in the black neighborhoods—for the black preacher or doctor or grocer.

Essentially, what black power is now saying in the North is that the North, too, should recognize that the middle-class occupations in the black neighborhoods belong to blacks, who are not permitted to hold such jobs in Italian, Polish, or other ethnic neighborhoods. The issue is phrased in terms of community power—that is to say, of giving to each neighborhood control over its own institutions—but this is tied inextricably to the distribution of middle-class jobs inside the neighborhood. It is unquestionably part of the American tradition that members of each ethnic group should be trained for the middle-class occupations in their neighborhoods, and that, given the training, they should have preference in employment in their own neighborhoods.

This kind of voluntary self-segregation has nothing in common with the compulsory segregation of other countries. An American neighborhood is not a ghetto. A ghetto is an area where members of an ethnic group are forced by law to live, and from which it is a criminal offense to emerge without the license of the oppressing power. This is what apartheid means in the Union of South Africa. An American neighborhood is not a place where members of an ethnic group are required by law to live; they may in the first instance have been forced to live there by circumstances, but it is soon transmuted, ideally, into a place where members of the group *choose* to live, and from which, ideally, anybody can emerge at any time that he wishes to do so. To confuse this neighborhood concept with apartheid is an egregious error.

The fundamental difference between apartheid and the American neighborhood comes out most clearly when one turns from what happens after 5 P.M. to what happens during the daytime. A neighborhood is a work place for less than half the community. The teachers, the doctors, the police, the grocers—these work where they live. But these people are supported by the labors of those who work in the factories and in other basic occupations outside the neighborhood. Some 50 to 60 per cent of the labor force moves out of the neighborhood every morning to work in the country's basic industries.

So a black strategy which concentrated exclusively on building up the black neighborhoods would be dealing with less than half the black man's economic problems. The neighborhood itself will not flourish unless the man who goes out of it in the morning brings back into it from the outside world an income adequate to support its institutions.

I wrote earlier that the American pattern is segregation in *social* life after 5 P.M. but integration in the *economic* life of the country during the day. American economic life is dominated by a few large corporations which do the greater part of the country's business; indeed, in manufacturing, half the assets of the entire country are owned by just 100 corporations. The world of these big corporations is an integrated world. There will be black grocery shops in black neighborhoods, but in your lifetime and mine there isn't going to be a black General Motors, a black Union Carbide, a black Penn-Central Railroad, or a black Standard Oil Company. These great corporations serve all ethnic groups and employ all ethnic groups. American economic life is inconceivable except on an integrated basis.

The majority of Afro-Americans work not in their neighborhoods but for one of the nonneighborhood corporations or employers, and so it shall be for as far ahead as we can see. The black problem is that while we are 11 per cent of the population, we have only 2 per cent of the jobs at the top, 4 per cent of the jobs in the middle, and are forced into 16 per cent of the jobs at the bottom—indeed into as much as 40 per cent of some of the jobs at the very bottom. Clearly, our minimum objective must be to capture 11 per cent of the jobs in the middle, and 11 per cent of the jobs at the top. Or, for those of us who have a pride in ourselves, it could even be an objective to have 15 per cent of the jobs at the top and in the middle, and only 8 per cent of those at the bottom, leaving the very bottom to less ambitious ethnic groups.

Not all our leaders understand that our central economic problem is not in the neighborhoods, but is in the fact that outside the neighborhoods, where most of us have to work, we are concentrated in the bottom jobs. For if they understood this they could not be as hostile as they are toward the black middle and upper classes. The measure of whether we are winning our battle is in how many of us rise to the middle and the top.

When a so-called militant abuses a successful Afro-American for having, by virtue of extreme hard work and immense self-discipline, managed to get to the top in the outside world, instead of devoting his energies to being—in the neighborhood —a social worker, or a night-school teacher, or a semi-politician, such a critic is merely being absurd. Rising from the bottom to the middle or the top, in the face of stiff white competition, prejudice and arbitrary barriers, takes everything that a man can give to it. It is our militants who should month-by-month chalk up the score of those who have broken through the barriers, should glory in their achievement, and should hold it up before our young to show them what black men can achieve.

Now, at last, I reach my central topic, which is the black man and the university. The road to the top in the great American corporations and other institutions is through higher education. Scientists, research workers, engineers, accountants, lawyers, financial administrators, Presidential advisers —all these people are recruited from the university. And indeed nearly all of the top people are taken from a very small number of colleges—from not more than some 50 or 60 of the 2,000 degree-granting institutions in the United States. The Afro-American could not make it to the top so long as he was effectively excluded from this small number of select institutions. The breakthrough of the Afro-American into these colleges is therefore absolutely fundamental to the larger economic strategy of black power.

I do not mean to suggest that the most important black strategy is to get more blacks into the best colleges. Probably the greatest contribution to black advancement would be to break the trade-union barriers which keep our people out of apprenticeships in the building and printing trades, and prevent our up-grading or promotion in other industries. The trade unions are the black man's greatest enemy in the United States.

The number of people who would be at the top, if we had our numerical share of the top, would be small. Our greatest task, in terms of numbers, is to conquer the middle—getting into skilled posts, foremen's posts, supervisory and white-collar jobs—through better use of apprenticeships, of the high schools and of technical colleges. I am going to discuss the universities not because this is numerically important, but partly because it has become so controversial, and partly because if we did conquer the top it would make much easier the conquering of the middle—both in our own minds, and in other people's minds, by altering our young people's image of themselves and of what they can achieve.

What can the good white college do for its black students that Howard or Lincoln or Fisk cannot do? It can open the road into the top jobs. It can do this only by giving our people the kinds of skills and the kind of polish which are looked for by people filling top jobs. To put it in unpopular language, it can train them to become top members of the establishment.

If it is wrong for young blacks to be trained for the top jobs in the big corporations, for top jobs in the government service, for ambassador-ships, for the editorial staff of The New York Times and so on—then there is little point in sending them to the best white colleges. On the contrary, if what one wants is people trained to live and work in black neighborhoods, they will do much better to go to the black colleges, of which there are, after all, more than 100, which know much better than Yale or Princeton or Dartmouth what the problems of black neighborhoods are, and how people should be trained to handle them. The point about the best white colleges is that they are a part, not of the neighborhood side of American life, but of the integrated part of American life, training people to run the economy and the administration in the integrated part of the day before 5 P.M.

But how can it be wrong for young Afro-Americans to be trained to hold superior positions in the integrated working world outside the neighborhood when in fact the neighborhood cannot provide work for even a half of its people? Whether we like it or not, most Afro-Americans *have* to work in the integrated world, and if we do not train for superior positions there, all that will happen is what happens now— that we shall be crowded into the worst-paid jobs.

If one grasps this point, that these 50 colleges are the gateway to the superior jobs, then the current attitudes of some of our black leaders to these colleges is not a little bewildering. In its most extreme form, what is asked is that the college should set aside a special part of itself which is to be the black part. There will be a separate building for black studies, and separate dormitories and living accommodations for blacks. There will be separate teachers, all black, teaching classes open only to blacks. The teachers are to be chosen by the students, and will for the most part be men whom no African or Indian or Chinese university would recognize as scholars, or be willing to hire as teachers.

Doubtless some colleges under militant pressure will give in to this, but I do not see what Afro-Americans will gain thereby. Employers will not hire the students who emerge from this process, and their usefulness even in black neighborhoods will be minimal.

I yield to none in thinking that every respectable university should give courses on African life and on Afro-American life, which are of course two entirely different subjects, and I am very anxious to see such courses developed. It is, however, my hope that they will be attended mostly by white students, and that the majority of black students will find more important uses for their time; that they may attend one or two such courses, but will reject any suggestion that black studies must be the major focus of their programs.

The principal argument for forcing black students to spend a great deal of their time in college studying African and Afro-American anthropology, history, languages and literature is that they need such studies to overcome their racial inferiority complex. I am not impressed by this argument. The youngster discovers that he is black around the age of 6 or 7; from then on, the whites he meets, the books he reads, and the situation of the Negro in America all combine to persuade him that he is an inferior species of Homo sapiens.

By the time he is 14 or 15 he has made up his mind on this one way or the other. Nothing that the college can do, after he reaches 18 or 19, is going to have much effect on his basic personality. To expect the colleges to eradicate the inferiority complexes of young black adults is to ask the impossible. And to expect this to come about by segregating black students in black studies under inferior teachers suggests some deficiency of thought.

Perhaps I am wrong about this. The proposition is essentially that the young black has been brainwashed into thinking himself inferior, so now he must spend four years in some place where he will be re-brainwashed into thinking himself equal. But the prospect that the 50 best colleges in the United States can be forced to take on this re-brainwashing operation is an idle dream. Those who are now putting all their energies into working for this are doomed to disappointment.

We are knocking our heads against the wrong wall. Every black student should learn some Afro-American history, and study various aspects of his people's culture, but the place for him to do this compulsorily is in the high school, and the best age to start this seriously is even earlier, perhaps around the age of 10. By the time the student gets to a first-rate college he should be ready for business—for the business of acquiring the skills which he is going to be able to use, whether in his neighborhood, or in the integrated economy. Let the clever young black go to a university to study engineering, medicine, chemistry, economics, law, agriculture and other subjects which are going to be of value to him and his people. And let the clever white go to college to read black novels, to learn Swahili, and to record the exploits of Negro heroes of the past. They are the ones to whom this will come as an eye-opener.

This, incidentally, is very much what happens in African universities. Most of these have well-equipped departments of African studies, which are popular with visiting whites, but very few African students waste their time (as they see it) on such studies, when there is so much to be learned for the jobs they will have to do. The attitude of Africans to their past conforms to the historian's observation that only decadent peoples, on the way down, feel an urgent need to mythologize and live in their past. A vigorous people, on the way up, has visions of its future, and cares next to nothing about its past.

My attitude toward the role of black studies in the education of college blacks derives not only from an unconventional view of what is to be gained therefrom, but also from an unconventional view of the purpose of going to college. The United States is the only country in the world which thinks that the purpose of going to colleges is to be educated. Everywhere else one goes to high school to be educated, but goes to college to be trained for one's life work. In the United States serious training does not begin until one reaches graduate school at the age of 22. Before that, one spends four years in college being educated—that is to say, spending 12 weeks getting some tidbits on religion, 12 weeks learning French, 12 weeks seeing whether the history professor is stimulating, 12 weeks seeking entertainment from the economics professor, 12 weeks confirming that one is not going to be able to master calculus, and so on.

If the purpose of going to college is to be educated, and serious study will not begin until one is 22, one might just as well, perhaps, spend the four years reading black novels, studying black history and learning to speak Fanti. But I do not think that American blacks can afford this luxury. I think our young people ought to get down to the business of serious preparation for their life work as soon after 18 as they can.

And I also note, incidentally, that many of the more intelligent white students are now in revolt against the way so many colleges fritter away their precious years in meaningless peregrination from subject to subject between the ages of 18 and 22.

Any Afro-American who wishes to become a specialist in black studies, or to spend some of his time on such work, should be absolutely free to do so. But I hope that, of those students who get the opportunity to attend the 50 best colleges, the proportion who want to specialize in black studies may, in their interest and that of the black community, turn out to be rather small, in comparison with our scientists, or engineers, accountants, economists or doctors.

Another attitude which puzzles me is that which requires black students in the better white colleges to mix only with each other; to have a dormitory to themselves; to eat at separate tables in the refectory, and so on. I have pointed out that these colleges are the gateway to leadership positions in the integrated part of the economy, and that what they can best do for young blacks is to prepare them to capture our 11 per cent share of the best jobs at the top—one of every nine ambassadorships, one of every nine vice-presidencies of General Motors, one of every nine senior directors of engineering laboratories, and so on.

Now I am told that the reason black students stick together is that they are uncomfortable in white company. But how is one to be Ambassador to Finland or Luxembourg—jobs which American Negroes have already held with distinction —if one is uncomfortable in white company? Anybody who occupies a supervisory post, from foreman upwards, is going to have white people working under him, who will expect him to be friendly and fair. Is this going to be possible, after four years spent in boycotting white company?

Nowadays in business and in government most decisions are made in committees. Top Afro-Americans cannot hope to be more than one in nine; they will always be greatly outnumbered by white people at their level. But how can one survive as the only black vice-president sitting on the executive committee of a large corporation if one is not so familiar with the ways and thoughts of other vice-presidents that one can even anticipate how they are going to think?

Blacks in America are inevitably and perpetually a minority. This means that in all administrative and leadership positions we are going to be outnumbered by white folks, and will have to compete with them not on our terms but on theirs. The only way to win this game is to know them so thoroughly that we can out-pace them. For us to turn our backs on this opportunity, by insisting on mingling only with other black students in college, is folly of the highest order.

This kind of social self-segregation is encouraged by two myths about the possibilities for black economic progress in the United States which need to be nailed. One is the Nixon myth, and the other, its opposite, is the revolutionary myth.

The first postulates that the solution is black capitalism—

to help as many blacks as possible to become big business-men. To be sure, it is feasible to have more successful small businesses operating inside the protection of the neighborhood—more grocers and drug stores and lunch counters; but I have emphasized that the members of every ethnic group mostly work outside their neighborhood in the integrated economy, buying from and selling to all ethnic groups. In this part of the economy the prospects for small business are bleak.

No doubt a few Negroes, born with the special talents which success in a highly competitive business world demands, will succeed in establishing sizable and highly competitive con-cerns. But the great majority who start on this road, whether white or black, go bankrupt in a short time. Indeed, about half of the new white businesses go bankrupt within the first 12 months. To tell the blacks that this is the direction in which they must move is almost a form of cruelty. To pretend that black America is going to be saved by the emergence of black capitalism, competing in the integrated economy with white capitalism, is little more than a hoax.

Neither is black America going to be saved by a Marxist revolution. Revolution takes power from one set of persons and gives it to another, but it does not change the hierarchical structure of the economy. Any kind of America that you can visualize, whether capitalist, communist, fascist, or any other kind of ist, is going to consist of large institutions like General Motors under one name or another. It will have people at the top, people in the middle and people at the bottom. Its leading engineers, doctors, scientists and administrators—leaving out a few top professional politicians—are going to be recruited from a small number of highly select colleges.

The problem of the black will essentially be the same—that problem being whether he is going to be mostly in the bottom jobs, or whether he will also get his 11 per cent share of the top and the middle. And his chance at the top is going to depend on his getting into those select schools and getting the same kind of technical training that the whites are getting—not some segregated schooling specially adapted for him, but the same kind that the whites get as their gateway to the top. Those black leaders who wish us to concentrate our efforts on working for revolution in America are living on a myth, for our problems and needed strategies are going to be exactly the same whether there is a revolution or not. In the integrated part of the American economy our essential strategy has to be to use all the normal channels of advancement—the high schools, the colleges, apprenticeships, night schools: It is only by climbing this ladder that the black man is going to escape from his concentration in the bottom jobs of the economy.

This is not, of course, simply a matter of schooling. The barriers of prejudice which keep us off the ladder still have to be broken down: the task of the civil-rights movement is still not completed, and we need all the liberal help, black and white, that we can get to help to keep the ladder clear. We need also to raise our own sights; to recognize that there are now more opportunities than there were, and to take every opportunity that offers. Here our record is good. For as the barriers came down in sports and entertainment, our young people moved swiftly to the top in baseball, football, the theater, or wherever else the road was cleared. We will do exactly the same in other spheres, given the opportunity.

The secret is to inspire our young people with confidence in their potential achievement. And psychologists tell us that the background to this is a warm and secure family life. The most successful minorities in America, the Chinese, the Japanese and the Jews, are distinguished by their close and highly disciplined family, which is the exact opposite of what has now become the stereotype of the white American family, with its undisciplined and uncontrollable children reared on what are alleged to be the principles of Dr. Spock. African families are warm, highly disciplined structures, just like Jewish or Chinese families. If black Americans are looking to Africa for aspects of culture which will distinguish them from white Americans, let them turn their backs on Spockism, and rear their children on African principles, for this is the way to the middle and the top. Given a disciplined family life and open doors to opportunity, I have no doubt that American blacks will capture one field after another, as fast as barriers come down.

The point which I have been trying to make is that the choice some of our leaders offer us between segregation and integration is false in the American context. America is integrated in the day and segregates itself at night. Some of our leaders who have just discovered the potential strength of neighborhood self-segregation have got drunk on it to the point of advocating segregation for all spheres of Afro-American life. But the struggle for community power in the neighborhood is not an alternative to the struggle for a better share of the integrated world outside the neighborhood, in which inevitably most of our people must earn their living. The way to a better share of this integrated economy is through the integrated colleges; but they can help us only if we take from them the same things that they give to our white competitors.

If we enter them merely to segregate ourselves in blackness, we shall lose the opportunity of our lives. Render homage unto segregated community power in the neighborhoods where it belongs, but do not let it mess up our chance of capturing our share of the economic world outside the neighborhood, where segregation weakens our power to compete.

Black Studies: An Intellectual Crisis

BY JOHN W. BLASSINGAME

John Blassingame, who teaches in the History Department at Yale University, was born in Georgia and received a B.S. from Fort Valley State College, M.A. from Howard University, and Ph.D. from Yale University. He has taught at Howard University and the University of Maryland and has served as Research Associate in Curriculum Development at Carnegie Mellon University and Assistant Editor of the Booker T. Washington Papers. He has written several articles on Negro troops in the Civil War, Southern History, and Latin American History. Contending that many of the Black Studies programs have been hastily organized with little commitment to excellence, Blassingame fears that too many of them are cruel hoaxes played on black students. Unlike Lythcott, he believes that the enthusiastic support by predominantly white colleges of black demands for segregated programs will lead to a recrudescence of "separate but equal" facilities for blacks. Though supporting Hare and Jordan's call for developing the black community, he questions whether this can be done through the contemporary Black Studies programs.

█T IS PRESUMPTUOUS of anyone to pretend to speak authoritatively on such a new development as black studies. At the end of a year fraught with the armed occupation of campus buildings and racial riots among students, I may rightfully be assigned to the camp of the foolhardy for attempting to speak on the rapidly escalating demands for increased attention to black people.

Black studies is such an emotionally loaded concept that

Reprinted by permission from *The American Scholar* XXXVIII (Autumn, 1969): 548–61.

most universities have had great difficulty in establishing programs. First of all, colleges started considering such programs at a time when the Negro community is furiously debating its place in American society. This, in itself, is not new. Generally, however, this is the first time that whites have seriously considered the debate worth noting. Consequently, they are often overwhelmed by the force of the demands, confused by the rhetoric, and unsure of the legitimate intellectual response.

The first problem that one encounters in surveying black studies programs around the country is the confusion over objectives. In fact, most people who write these proposals never include objectives, goals or the justification for such programs. Instead, such ambiguous terms as "need," "demand," "relevance," or "such a program needs no justification" are used. It is inconceivable that any other kind of program could be established with so little thought being given to long-range goals. When I have asked college teachers around the country why they are establishing black studies, the usual answer has been that the black students demand them. When I ask black students what are the goals of Afro-American studies, I often get a blank stare. In one committee meeting on black studies as a university in Washington, D.C., a Negro student demanded that thirty new courses be offered next year and a black studies department be created. When a faculty member asked what the objectives of the department would be, the student replied, "How do you expect me, a freshman, to know?" and stormed out of the conference room.

There is often great confusion over objectives and contradictory patterns in the programs. Reacting to student demands for "relevance," a number of colleges have combined social service concepts with traditional academic pursuits. In spite of the fact that neither students nor faculty know what the students mean by "relevance," some effort is made to give students some contact with, or skills they can ostensibly carry back to, the black community. Few of them try to find out what the black community thinks is "relevant" to its needs. Then, too, such an objective clearly reveals other inconsistencies in goals. Although established at predominantly white universities apparently for all students, no consideration is given to the "relevance" of the programs to the white community. Of course, some blacks and whites argue that such programs are intended solely for Negro students.

Black students have demanded that black studies, above all else, should be "relevant" to their needs. As far as one can determine, the programs are supposed to give them pride, a sense of personal worth, and the tools for restructuring society. The attempts to fulfill the last objective are often the most confusing and contradictory aspects of the programs. Rarely is there much thought about what is needed to restructure society. Many students apparently forget that it is still true that the first requirement in any struggle is to know your enemy. What blacks need more than anything else is much more sophisticated knowledge about American society. It is not enough to know that "whitey" has been, and is, oppressing blacks; most Negroes do not have to go to college to learn that. Instead, Negroes must study business practices, high finance, labor law and practices, judicial procedures, consumer practices and the communications media.

Armed with this knowledge, blacks would know which of the interlocking corporations to boycott or buy stock in to bring about meaningful change in their economic position. Knowledge of labor unions may enable blacks to break down the almost invulnerable conspiracy to prevent blacks from earning a living that is based on the tripod of nepotism, political corruption, and prejudice. With serious study we may learn that injunctions, boycotts, campaigns for open shops in union states, government-operated apprenticeship programs, application of conspiracy laws, and other devices may force the unions to loosen their stranglehold on the black worker. While a study of the law may convince us that it is a device for oppression of the poor, we may find enough loopholes in it to afford some degree of protection to the weak. Investigation of law enforcement practices may permit Americans to regain civilian control over our quasi-military, autonomous police. A clearer understanding of the communications media may enable us not only to increase black representation in the publishing, radio, television and advertising fields, but to change white attitudes toward blacks and to create a more favorable image of blacks in the communications media. These are the things that are most "relevant" to the black community.

For many white colleges, faced with the demand to lower admission standards to take in more black students, black studies represents a "soft" program that these students can pass. While I believe that it is criminal for any college to admit poorly prepared students without establishing academic support programs to help them, I do not think there is any predominantly white college that has the experience or the will to do this. If they are serious in their endeavors to establish academic support programs for poorly prepared students, they will have to turn for advice to predominantly Negro colleges, which have had a great deal more experience in this area. Even so, a program that lacks academic respectability is of no use at all to black students and is certainly irrelevant to the black community.

The reasoning behind many of the black studies programs is more sinister than I have indicated. It is clear that in many cases predominantly white schools have deliberately organized ill-conceived programs because they are intended solely for Negro students. In short, a number of institutions are not seriously committed to Afro-American studies. Some professors at one of the leading universities in the country will approve, without question, any proposal for black studies because they say "it's only for the niggers." At a time when most traditional departments in state universities find it difficult to operate on a million dollar annual budget, black studies programs are established with a budget of less than a quarter of a million dollars to use for teaching personnel *and* a plethora of community action programs. Many colleges are not seriously committed to black studies because they feel the demand will die out shortly. Consequently, rather than setting aside university funds to establish the programs, they turn to foundations for support. This, of course, is not conducive to long-term planning. As our experience with Latin American studies reveals, the cycle of foundation interest in such programs is, at most, ten years. The cycle for black studies, I predict, will be even shorter. The foundation money is likely to dry up very quickly when Mao Tse-tung perfects his intercontinental ballistic missile—then, we will embark on Chinese studies.

The lack of commitment extends beyond inadequate financial support to far more serious realms. The most serious is the elimination of any required standards for teachers. While I accept many of the complaints against the traditional academic degrees, it is clear that Urban League officials and local black preachers are not, in very many cases, prepared to teach the college level courses in black studies that they have been assigned. Similarly, while I share the general arrogance of college teachers who feel they can teach anything in their general field, it is too late for most of us to retool quickly to teach topics we have ignored for twenty and thirty years. Yet, because of the lack of commitment and the urgent demand, many colleges are hiring all manner of people to teach black-oriented courses, especially if they are black. Social workers, graduate students who have just embarked on their graduate careers, high school teachers, principals, and practically anyone who looks black or has mentioned Negroes in an article, book or seminar paper are hired to teach Afro-American courses.

These poorly prepared teachers are hired in some cases to discredit the whole program. Given such teachers and in the face of such designs, black and white students are justified in running the teachers out of the classrooms as they have done in many cases.

Generally, Negro students have demanded that black instructors teach black-oriented courses. In many ways I sympathize with them. Having faced unprepared white teachers who have sometimes had to get their reading lists from the black students and who have not learned that Negro is spelled with an "e" instead of an "i," the black students are skeptical. Besides, they reason, it was the white scholar who, by his writing and teaching, made the Negro the "invisible man" of American scholarship. It is certainly asking a lot to expect one to accept cheerfully a man who has continuously embezzled from him his pride, culture, history and manhood for more than four hundred years.

In spite of these considerations, the black students often go too far. All white teachers are not racists. I submit that some of them have more "soul" than some blacks. "Blackness," in all its shades, represents no mystical guarantee of an "understanding" of the black man's problems, life or culture. Neither color nor earnestness but training must be the test applied to any teacher. Since many black students suffer from contact earlier with poorly trained teachers, it is more of a disservice to them than to white students to add more ill-prepared instructors at the last stage of their education. Yet, in their fervor to find black teachers, Negro students ignore the possible crippling effects of hiring simply *any* black man. They have often suggested teachers whom no administrator, regardless of his designs, could accept. For example, a group of black students in one college suggested that a Negro graduate student who had not completed a year of graduate study be hired to teach a Negro history course. Upon investigation, it was discovered that the student in question had already flunked out of graduate school during the first semester.

The black students, however, must be applauded for forcing predominantly white colleges to come to grips with their discriminatory hiring practices. Still, the revolution in this area will fall short if Negro students only demand black teachers for black-oriented subjects. Instead, they must broaden their demands into other areas. How many blacks do we have teaching mathematics, biology, engineering or law at predominantly white schools? Faculty desegregation must expand into these areas if the black scholar is not to end up in an intellectual straitjacket where he is restricted to black-oriented subjects.

The threat to black intellectuals is real. Not only do the black students demand that the teachers in black studies programs be Negroes, they also want them to have the right shade of "blackness." In essence, this means that the black scholar must have the right ideological leanings. As some of us succumb to the persuasive arguments to hop on the treadmill and try to keep up with the mercurial changes in the black "party line," serious scholarship is likely to suffer. It is in this regard that the control of black studies programs by black students is most dangerous. Black scholars being considered for positions in these programs must not only gain the approval by the faculty of their academic credentials, they must also kowtow to the black students. On one occasion a friend of mine, after receiving faculty approval of his appointment at one college, was required to pay obeisance to the black students. Flamboyant by nature, he went home, donned flowing African robes, returned, wowed the students and received the appointment. The case of another black scholar was more tragic. After being approved by the faculty, he went before the black students to prove his ideological fitness. When he opened his remarks to them by pointing out that he had a white wife, the students rejected him. In spite of his qualifications he was not hired.

I do not mean to imply by the preceding remarks that I reject student involvement in decisions that affect their lives. On the contrary, I feel that we must do much more in this direction. In no case, however, should student control go so far as to restrict the intellectual freedom of the scholar. Even if one wants to push "black realism," this is not the way to do it. Black intellectuals have worked so long and hard in their fight against the white intellectual establishment, often publishing their own books when white publishers rejected them because they were unorthodox, that they do not want manumission from their white masters only to be enslaved by black masters. In short, while we support student involvement, we reject it for black studies until the same degree of student control is extended to other areas.

Often, when the Negro scholar escapes the ideological snare of the black students, he faces the almost equally dangerous trap of being overworked by his white colleagues. Frequently, because he is one of few blacks on the faculty, presidents and deans use him as a flying troubleshooter to defang militant students. Inevitably, he is appointed to every committee that is related in any way to Negroes (and the list of them seems limitless). Then, too, the Negro scholar is expected to serve as father-confessor, counselor, success model, substitute parent, general dispenser of pablum to overwrought black students, and all-around authority on the "Negro problem." Consequently, the Negro scholar finds himself more overworked than when he taught fifteen hours a week in a predominantly Negro school. The danger in all of this is that black scholars may find that they have almost no time for research and writing. Few students and administrators realize that by requiring an inordinate amount of work from black scholars they are seriously crippling them in their efforts to find out more about the black experience.

Few students seem to realize that their demands for black faculty are causing raids of major proportions on the faculties of Negro colleges. Of course, some students have insisted that their schools raid only other white colleges. The impact of the current raiding practices (and they are likely to increase) on the Negro colleges is not clear. On the one hand, predominantly white colleges are finding that it is not easy to entice Negro faculty away from places they have been for several years. Many black professors disdain the offers because they do not feel the predominantly white colleges will follow through later on promotions. Others argue that they were told to go and teach "their people" ten years ago and to hell with the white schools that have suddenly discovered them. Where were they ten years ago when they were really needed? Many black professors refuse the offers because they realize that their white colleagues will not respect their academic credentials.

In spite of all the hue and cry from black college administrators, the raids have had a salutary effect on the position of the black faculty member. Deans are suddenly discovering that they can add $5,000 to an instructor's salary at the same time that they cut his teaching load by six hours. Since he is now the rarest gem in the academic marketplace, the black teacher is rapidly approaching parity with his white colleagues in the perquisites of the profession. In many cases, black administrators have used the raiding as a lever to pry more money out of reluctant state legislatures for teaching salaries.

The demands of black students for separate, autonomous black studies departments, separate social centers and dormitories have been a godsend to white racists engulfed by the liberal wave of the last ten years. Ivy League Ku Klux Klansmen applaud and vigorously support such demands. The immediate capitulation of white colleges to such demands is understandable: they support their traditional beliefs and practices. Take Harvard, for example. When a Negro graduate of Harvard, Roscoe Conkling Bruce, tried to reserve a room in the freshman dormitory for his son in 1923, President A. Lawrence Lowell refused the request. He wrote Bruce: "I am sorry to have to tell you that in the freshman halls we have felt from the beginning the necessity of excluding Negroes. I am sure you will understand why we have thought it impossible to compel the two races to live together." In April of the same year the Board of Overseers of Harvard voted unanimously that "men of the white and Negro races shall not be compelled to live together."

By endorsing the shibboleths of "self-determination," many white intellectuals are really supporting a recrudescence of "separate but equal" facilities. In this regard, black students can appreciably close the generation gap by asking their parents what separate facilities mean in practice. Few of them have forgotten that a separate railroad car meant uncomfortable, dilapidated, filthy, rarely cleaned cars where black women were insulted by drunken white hooligans. Separate residential areas meant, and still do mean, unventilated, rarely heated, overcrowded, unpainted apartments with high rents, few city services, consistent violation of housing codes by unfeeling landlords who go unpunished by city officials, and black men and women dying of tuberculosis and in firetraps, and black babies dying from rat bites.

When it has been possible for whites to give Negroes separate educational facilities, this has been done with enthusiasm. The result has always been disastrous. Separate facilities have never been equal. It is incomprehensible that black students can trust what they call the "white power structure" to provide separate but equal facilities at the same time that the current administration, as conservative as it is, has found that several Southern states are still offering separate but unequal education to blacks and whites. The evidence of this is overwhelming. A cursory check of state expenditures to black and white colleges supports the charge. How can blacks receive an equal education in Florida when the state expenditures for white colleges were twenty-seven times larger than appropriations for Negro colleges in 1963? For those who eschew research, an on-the-site investigation would be instructive. Who can compare the small cinderblock buildings of Southern University in New Orleans with the shiny, commodious brick buildings of Louisiana State University right down the street and believe that separate facilities can be equal?

Are predominantly white colleges any more justified in bowing to the demand of black students for separate social facilities and black roommates than they are for bowing to the same demands of white students? The answer is an unequivocal no. Instead, they must react the way Columbia University did in 1924 when a group of white students threatened to leave a dormitory because a Negro student was admitted. Dean Hawkes spoke for the faculty when he asserted:

"If any student finds his surroundings uncongenial, there is no need for him to stay in Farnald Hall or anywhere else at the University."

I understand the very persuasive arguments of many black students that they need these separate facilities for emotional reinforcement. I sympathize with them but reject their argument. I have read too many autobiographies of black men who studied at white institutions when racism was much more violently overt and when they were much more deprived educationally and culturally than any of these students are, to accept their facile arguments. Often the lone student at Yale, Harvard, Oberlin, Iowa State and other colleges, these men succeeded in spite of the lack of organized programs of emotional reinforcement.

A number of predominantly white colleges have not only utilized black studies to set up separate social facilities for blacks, they have also organized all-black classes for their Negro students. When the black students at a California college complained that they were being used as resource persons in a "Racism in America" course, a separate all-black section was established with a black psychologist as the teacher. The reaction of the students to the course was mixed. One group told me that it was a great course because the teacher required no reading; allegedly, since all of the blacks understood white racism, they simply met and "rapped" with each other. The more astute students described the course as a "bull session" where everybody "got down on whitey."

While some California schools have retrograded further than most colleges, many of the others are not far behind. Even when these programs have been open to all students, the belligerent attitudes of the black students have often scared white students away. To the historian all of this is reminiscent of the treatment of black students when many white schools were first desegregated. Many contemporary black students are in these colleges because earlier black men were not even allowed in the classroom with their white classmates when they desegregated white colleges. Is it fair to the memory of men like this for black students to turn their college educations into "bull sessions" that they could have had without going to college?

Inadvertently, the white colleges are reinforcing the growth of apartheid in America, denying black and white students the opportunity to learn to understand all people, and approving the denial of social equality to Negroes. America's predominantly white colleges can follow one of two paths. The current separatist ideologies fostered by black studies plans can only lead to more Negro students feeling like one black Columbia University student who wrote in 1967: "I feel compelled to announce the fact that Columbia College will never be integrated. If half, or even three-quarters of the College population were black, there would still exist two separate and basically unrelated student communities . . ." Another student at Columbia indicated the other direction. He asserted that at Columbia, "Acutely aware of the white-problem-in-America as I am, as prejudiced toward my own people as I am, I have still found individuals—not black—whom I can respect, admire, and even love."

I realize that any new program may initially encounter many problems. Those that I outlined above, however, can be avoided. The Negro community has too much at stake—its very existence—for the college community, again, to miss an opportunity to begin to end the centuries of neglect and repression of blacks in America. Black studies is too serious an intellectual sphere, has too many exciting possibilities of finally liberating the racially shackled American mind, for intellectuals to shirk their responsibility to organize academically

respectable programs. This possibility of curricular innovation must not be used to establish totally different programs,
segregated entirely from traditional schemes. Instead, we must
take advantage of this opportunity to enrich the educational
experiences of all students and teach them to think and to
understand more clearly the problems of their age. While we
may make our admissions procedures more logical in an effort
to find more Negro students, they must be required, whether
in black studies or in any other program, to meet the requirements that all other students must meet to graduate. The black
community has suffered too much already from the "Negro
degrees" given to us in the past by predominantly white
colleges.

I do not mean to imply by the remarks made above that the
growing maze of black studies programs has been developed
only for sinister reasons. In all probability most of the individuals establishing and supporting them have been sincere.
But goaded by the emotional demands of black students and
pushed by a growing sense of guilt at having fiddled while
America burned, many white intellectuals have organized instant programs of little worth. Characteristically, intellectuals,
frustrated by their inactive lives, often want to propose fuzzy
plans for the immediate eradication of ills. In this instance
they have been hamstrung by two things. On the one hand, the
guilt they feel for having contributed to the perpetuation of
racism in America causes them to clutch frantically at any
straw that may atone for their sins. On the other, they are
forced by the masterful rhetorical play on this guilt by black
students to accept the most far-reaching and often unworkable
plans for a total restructuring of American society. The key
to the dilemma is the rhetoric of the black students.

Adopting the classic political technique of demanding
more than one is willing to accept, black students discovered

very quickly that white intellectuals actually believed that their demands were nonnegotiable. Consequently, white intellectuals have established programs that are, in many instances, practically closed to white students, are soothing to their consciences because they seek to provide services to the black community that only the state can provide, are organized and controlled by students, are contrary to the logical pattern of existing programs, are based solely on emotional rather than intellectual needs, are designed to perpetuate the white myth that Negroes cannot compete on an equal basis, are suited to contemporary problems rather than equipping students to propose new solutions to the ever-changing nature of proscriptions against blacks in America, and permit Negroes to learn about themselves at the expense of knowledge about the larger American society with which they must battle. Such programs represent poor preparation indeed for black men who must survive in a white society.

The most serious effect of student rhetoric on black studies programs is undoubtedly the white acceptance of the demand for combining community action, academic and counseling programs. I agree with the students that the university cannot fulfill its *raison d'être* by ignoring community needs. Similarly, I feel that some students, in the best tradition of Rousseau, should have firsthand knowledge of the community in which they live. To provide this through community action programs is, of course, an enormous undertaking. A few years ago when Howard University officials adopted a community action program for the Washington census tract with the worst social problems, they found that the $400,000 they invested in the program made little impact. The problems encountered in our mini-war on poverty are also instructive in this regard. The poverty program with its well-meaning, paternalistic, relatively well-financed activities has not only in many cases been less than beneficial, but has often been positively destructive, to the black community. In light of the desire of blacks to "do their own thing," how are we to react to another series of paternalistic programs directed by people in the so-called "white power structure"?

Such programs can, of course, be highly successful. First, however, they must be much more carefully planned than most of those I have seen. One gets the vague impression upon reading many of the proposals that a horde of idealistic black, and maybe white, students are going to be let loose on the black community. Black men and women have played in this scene many times before. Nothing could be more self-defeating. A short time ago I watched a team of young, highly committed, but wholly undirected VISTA workers unintentionally insult blacks in their first public contact with them in a small rural Louisiana community. In light of the tensions in urban areas, community action programs must be well organized, carefully planned, and amply funded. They must, in addition, involve community leaders in the initial planning stages of the programs.

One question that apparently never arises in connection with this aspect of black studies proposals is how much community involvement students actually want. Are contemporary students *that* different from those of my own generation? Do they really have that much time after studying? In many cases investigation has shown that at the same time that students demand more community action programs they rarely participate in those that the colleges have already established.

While the lack of serious thought behind many of these programs can be hidden by skipping over objectives and using glittering generalities in regard to the community action arm, all of the confusion, guilt and sinister designs are revealed in the list of courses. All of the proposals begin by hiding the colleges' sins behind grandiose claims about the number of black-oriented or related courses they already offer. Many of these are often very tangentially related to blacks under the broadest conception possible. The revelations about the nature of the programs, however, are in the new courses. I realize the variations on a black theme may be endless, but I am frankly amazed as I read the list of some new courses. While it may be possible to teach a course on the "Afro-American on the Frontier." I have serious doubts about the course proposed for one black studies program entitled "The Sociology of Black Sports." And although we have done very little research on the Negro family, it may be possible to teach a course on the subject. But can we, as one college proposes, offer one course on "The Black Family in the Urban Environment" and another one on "The Black Family in the Rural Environment"? What in the world is the course proposed in a California state college entitled "Relevant Recreation in the Ghetto"? This same school must have had a deeply disturbed home economist on its black studies committee, for it also proposed that one of the relevant courses for the Afro American program should be "The Selection and Preparation of Soul Food."

That delectable tidbit indicates clearly the slim intellectual base of many programs. Even when the programs have not been this shallow, they have often been planned with little thought of what is going on in the American educational establishment. The contemporary revolution in public school textbooks, the burgeoning summer institutes, and rapid changes in public school offerings are bound to catch up with many college-level black studies programs in the next few years. The number of courses one takes is irrelevant if the reading list and general information are the same as that one received in high school. After all, the thrill of hearing Crispus

Attucks praised in the first grade, rediscovered in the eighth, revived in the twelfth, and finally "evaluated" in college is just as deadening as our annual peregrinations with Columbus. Dry rot is already surfacing in some programs. Some students find that the "Introductory Seminar in Afro-American Studies" often exhausts the books and articles the teachers in their other courses are able to find. Strangely enough, the reading list for the "Sociology of Race Relations" is often identical to the one for "The Afro-American in American History." The toleration level of students for this kind of shallowness is understandably low.

While all of the problems I have indicated place black studies in serious jeopardy, they are not insurmountable. To overcome these obstacles we have to plot new courses for black studies. First, the programs should be rationally organized, fitted into the total pattern of university offerings, be directed to the needs of all students, amply funded, and as intellectually respectable as any other college program. The same qualifications should be required of teachers, the same work of students, and there should be clearly stated objectives, as there are in other academic programs. Community action programs must be separated from academic programs and adequately financed, staffed and truly related to community needs. Finally, if any of these programs is to succeed, we must break out of our airtight cage of guilt and emotionalism to the open arena where we can establish a meaningful dialogue on black studies.

PART THREE

Black History and Culture

Black Culture/
White Teacher

BY CATHARINE R. STIMPSON

Catharine Stimpson teaches at Barnard College. Drawing on her class-room experiences, Stimpson contends that white readers do not under-stand black literature except on a shallow level which provides them with emotional kicks or expiates their guilt. White critics, she argues, are blind to the linguistic complexities of black literature and try to fit it into the mold of sterile white literature. The white teacher who understands black writers must rebel against the values of his white world. So few are able to do this that the only people qualified to teach black literature are blacks.

MOST WHITE PEOPLE misread black literature, if they read it at all. Their critical twistings are still another symptom of the dominant attitude toward black people and black culture in America. The white ego insists upon control. Not only do white readers demand that black literature satisfy their needs and notions, but they literally read it according to them. They have trouble, to paraphrase James Baldwin, getting off its back.

Some readers use black literature politically—to condemn Western history and white racism, and to earn credit from a would-be revolutionary future. An Eldridge Cleaver be-comes their surrogate rebel leader: bombastic, schematic, vicious to homosexuals, unfair to white women, but a rhetori-cal broom for change. Exploiting black writers, such readers

Reprinted by permission from *Change*, May–June, 1970, pp. 35–40.

evade responsibility: applauding an outraged minority takes the place of dealing with a disagreeable silent majority.

Other white readers, even the most sophisticated of them, use black literature emotionally—for kicks, for a "primitive" energy lost or missing from their own lives. In Ralph Ellison's words, they "seem to feel that they can air with impunity their most private Freudian fantasies as long as [the fantasies] are given the slightest camouflage of intellectuality and projected as 'Negro.' They have made of the no-man's-land created by segregation a territory for infantile self-expression and intellectual anarchy." Unfortunately, these readers go on to dismiss their black savants of the nitty-gritty at their whim. They make one race both sage and scapegoat. The brief history of white affection for black writers during the Harlem Renaissance in the 1920s is a paradigm of such behavior.

Still other readers use black literature for intellectual capital. Some, for example, read it as evidence that an alien culture supports the ideas and values of the dominant culture. To these people, the black writer may be a renegade and prophet, but the vision he forges in the smithy of his soul is a familiar one. Such readers, though, find the new black voices confusing. Others use black writing to dig out information about an alien culture. They recognize that some black writers, like Ellison, work with symbols, but usually they think of black artists as naturalists, and they look to them for reports about a scene they could themselves never view. Yet their sense of naturalism does not coincide with true black naturalism—the kind, for instance, of Ed Bullins, the playwright; white commentators, like Walter Kerr, call them rhetorical, overblown, or inaccurate.

Some readers, of course, have more than one of these tendencies. When Robert Bone says, "Like any other artist, the Negro novelist must achieve universality through a sensitive interpretation of his own culture," he is insisting that black literature be a document which conforms to Bone's own critical ideology.[1] The white readers of black literature have a good deal in common. The pressure of the past, fear, and vanity make them like protest fiction, which, no matter how grim or didactic, appeals to them. It says that to be black is to be miserable: being black is worse than being white. Protest fiction massages guilt. *If I read Native Son, I must be all right.* It titillates a sense of justice. *If I read Native Son, my moral faculties are alert.* It offers an underworld tour. *If I read Native Son, I'm really getting data about tenements and rats.* Protest themes, like those of "passing" or of the tragic mulatto, also flatter whites. Black murderer Bigger Thomas may be the putative protagonist of *Native Son,* and murderous white capitalism the villain, but the hero is Max: a lawyer, a white.

My ideas about black literature were put together in an urban college classroom the color of a stale yellow legal pad. I was teaching a course called "Books and the Black Experience in America." There were twenty-five students, all girls, mostly middle class, nineteen of them white, six black, all of them sitting tensely together. History has made geniality improbable.

I would prefer not to teach that class again. White people at the moment have neither the intellectual skill nor the emotional clarity nor the moral authority to lead the pursuit of

---

[1] Bone is an erudite, sympathetic, and helpful critic. However, he shows not only a white tendency toward *ex cathedra* pronouncements but also the way in which whites have been preferred to blacks as critics of black literature. His book, *The Negro Novel in America,* printed in 1958, was reprinted and revised in 1965. By 1968 it had gone through five printings. In contrast, Sterling Brown's encyclopedic *The Negro in American Fiction,* issued in 1937, languished until 1968, when the small Kennikat Press in Port Washington, New York, reissued it.

black studies. Race, to the dismay of many, to the relief of others, has become a proper test for deciding who is best at certain intellectual, as well as political, activities, and teaching black literature is one of them.

I want to keep reading black literature, though. What matters is reading it accurately. And doing that demands a new, practical, literary theory for white people.

White readers cling to mutually contradictory stereotypes: the Black as Militant; the Black as Struggling, Suffering Sacrifice; the Black as Sambo; the Black as Beast; the Black as White (Almost); the Black as the Hot Time in the Old Bed Tonight. This confusion marks not simply the ordinary jumble of the human mind but an oppressive mode of reading based on contempt. It reveals white ignorance about the idiosyncrasies, the idioms, the intricacy, and the integrity of the black experience. Whites, trying to dispel their ignorance, often become patronizing or politically desperate.

One day a black student came to my office. "I can't take that girl any longer," she said, naming an earnest but naïve and bossy white student. "I'm tired of being asked how I do my Afro and how I dance."

"Come on," I said, "she doesn't really say those things, does she?"

She did.

In class the next day a white student asked the black students, "How does it feel to be black?" An attractive and highly intelligent black senior replied, "I'm here to learn, not to educate you."

The white students were angered. They had assumed the privilege of instant understanding. "How can we learn if you don't tell us?"

"Try reading the books," they were told.

White witlessness about the black oral tradition is a particular source of misreading. Whites tend to ignore, despise or steal from rich, figurative black speech. Or they call it the language of the ghetto, the deprived, the folk. Yet black literature uses it in addition to the more conventional American public speech. Black language seems neither esoteric, like the mumbo-jumbo of a cult; nor heavy, like interoffice memoranda; nor jargonish, like faculty chitchat. Rather, it seems subtle, precise, vibrant. Its speaker, as much leader or performer as speaker, possesses both formal oratorical power and spontaneous wit. Often the word is part of a stylized game, like the dozens, or of a dramatic pattern, like the call-and-response. Perhaps the deep structure of black language is African. Certainly its texture reflects the slave experience in America:

> When black people were brought to America [Mike Thelwell, the black writer, says] they were deprived of their language and of the underpinnings in cultural experience out of which a language comes. It is clear that they developed two languages, one for themselves and another for the white masters. . . . The only vestiges we can find of the real language of the slaves are in the few spirituals which have come down to us. . . . It is a language produced by oppression, but one whose central impulse is survival and resistance. . . . It depends on what linguists call para-language; that is, gesture, physical expression and modulation of all cadences and intonation which serve to change the meaning—in incredibly subtle ways—of the same collection of words. It is intensely poetic and expressive.[2]

Nor are white readers blind and deaf only to the linguistic complexity of black literature. Their ignorance of the realities

---

[2] From "Back With the Wind," in *William Styron's Nat Turner: Ten Black Writers Respond,* edited by John Hendrik Clarke. Copyright © 1968 by Beacon Press.

of American history is equally troublesome. They know George Washington, George Wallace, and precious little in between. Free falling in the intellectual emptiness are some myths, called history, and some illusions, called myth. Such American ahistoricity is a paradox. Americans tend to be possessive; they like to get, to keep, and get more of things; possessive people are usually conservative; conservative people usually study history—they feel they are clutching time itself. The American distaste for even an informal knowledge of the past may be defensive. Certainly it protects most white readers from grasping the bloodier experiences which black literature reflects, the daily effort it has made to preserve and to transform itself, the many ironic strategies it successfully deploys, and the intensity of the moral passion it so frequently emits.

My class was reading Frederick Douglass's Narrative *of his life to 1845. Most of the white students had a strange notion of slavery. Many still seemed to believe in Tara. "Where were you all those years you were going to school?" a black student finally asked. "When you saw those pictures of the cotton fields, who'd you think all those people were out there in those handkerchiefs?"*

Another day we were reading Booker T. Washington's autobiography, Up from Slavery, *which includes his famous address to the Atlanta Exposition in 1895. There the ambiguous, proud, wily leader praised white strength and black labor. To white cheers and black silence he promised law, order and social segregation. We called Booker T. a disaster, an Uncle Tom. But a black student contradicted us. "Booker T. knew what he was doing," she said. "He was speaking in Atlanta. He was running a school in the Black Belt just after Reconstruction. He was doing what he had to do to keep his people alive."*

One of the most romantic modern myths makes the artist a prophet. He lightens our dark corners, bears witness to suffering, and rebukes vulgarity and evil. But most whites who write about blacks betray the myth: far too often they are accomplices of racism. Some white writers, to be sure, are more honorable than others. Lillian Smith is more compassionate than the repellent Margaret Mitchell, Harriet Beecher Stowe more righteous than Thomas Dixon, a P.R. man for the Ku Klux Klan. However, even the best of black characters created by white writers function within white contexts. They objectify white notions, values, ambitions, theatricalities, anxieties, and besetting fears. William Styron's Nat Turner—Dark Hued Screw-Up, Vengeful then Repentant Onanist, Lusting after White Flesh—dramatizes not black rebellion but Styron's quasi-Freudian, quasi-existential vision of history. As white writers bear down upon their black characters, they seem to impose a weight that is heavier and more masterful than the one they commonly impose. Further, they betray a liberal function of art: to take into strict account the otherness of others.

White ideas about black literature are more than private fancies. They are also embedded in public institutions which, if more open today than they once were, are still relatively closed to black people. (The *American Literary Anthology*, to take one example, which has government support, publishes some black writers, but it has neither black editors nor black judges.) For moral, psychological, political, aesthetic and practical reasons, many blacks have written to influence or to please those institutions. They have made much of their work conform to white expectations. White audiences have been able to let their errors about black people harden into habit. Black audiences have often been alienated. This is, in part, what Arna Bontemps means when he says, ". . . the Negro reader has little taste for any art in which the racial attitudes of the past are condoned or taken for granted. . . . This is what he has come to expect in the fiction in which he sees himself."

Paul Laurence Dunbar, born in 1872, died a tubercular drunk in 1906. The first professional black writer in America, he was economically dependent on a white audience. He wrote two kinds of poetry: traditional formal verse, which he liked, and Negro dialect verse, which he sold. He used white culture to describe his own black experience, and black culture to describe a white notion of black experience. Skillfully, if unhappily, he mirrored for his audience their deluded fantasies of an old South in which the masters were benevolent and the happy, happy darkies wished Mistah Lincum would "tek his freedom back." Dunbar's white patron, William Dean Howells, reveals how whites treat black writers. In an introduction for Dunbar, Howells dismisses the traditional verse, but he praises the dialect poems: ". . . divinations and reports of what passes in the hearts and minds of a lowly people whose poetry had hitherto been inarticulately expressed in music, but now finds, for the first time in our tongue, literary interpretation of a very artistic completeness."

Many of Howell's phrases, such as "our tongue," are beguiling: Big Massa will bless Emerging Talent, if the price is right. Howells was perhaps the first to make a black writer a "vogue," to borrow a term from Langston Hughes. Ironically, some of the most insidious harm white readers have done to black literature has been through excessive praise of one person. Nearly every decade has had one (and rarely more than one) house nigger in the library of art. To him all praises flow. *Look,* white readers say, *that boy sure can write.*

Obviously, not every black writer writes for the white audience. Many new, brilliant black writers, like some of their ancestors of the Harlem Renaissance, work for blacks. They ignore the whites, whose needs and pleasures they find irrelevant at best. The whites then feel rejected. (It is unlikely that whites, no matter how much they read, will ever really share the new black consciousness.) Other black writers, like many whites, shrug off the separation of readers into racial camps. Some think it contrary to the spirit of art; others think it contrary to the spirit of integration. Still others believe that education, geography, taste and class divide readers more accurately than color. Still others say the whole question is of only momentary urgency. In a while, they claim, asking for whom Chester Himes wrote *Pinktoes* will have the same urgency as asking for whom Shakespeare wrote *Macbeth*—King James or the boys down at the Globe.

Yet the black writer's conception of his audience influences his writing as pressure does mercury. (I suspect that black literature falls into two categories: books written mostly for blacks and books written mostly for whites—which must often include explanatory detail about black customs.) When the writer takes his audience seriously, he assumes his work will *do* something, not as a crystal ball hanging in the void, but as a force for better or worse which has been someplace and is going somewhere. White readers generally overlook this purposeful quality of black literature. Yet breaking the back of colonialism and liberating a people call for a literature of content, and literary questions become more than exercises. Answering them means resolving political, racial and ethical problems. For the black writer today it also means being accountable to the black community. As Eldridge Cleaver has said, "The next group we [the Panthers] are going to have to move against . . . are these black writers. . . . Before it wasn't important what they wrote because black people weren't reading what they said anyhow. But now black people are reading and it's important what is being written."

One morning I extravagantly praised Black Boy *as a narrative of rebellion, exile and flight. "I can't accept what you say," a black student said. "Richard Wright debases black people. He has no sense of the community. How can you fall all over* Black Boy *when it has passages like this: '. . . after the habit of reflection had been born in me, I used to mull over the strange absence of real kindness in Negroes, how unstable was our tenderness, how lacking in genuine passion we were, how void of great hope, how timid our joy, how bare our traditions, how hollow our memories, how lacking we were in those intangible sentiments that bind man to man, and how shallow was even our despair'?"*

How indeed should we judge a book? Because of its "art" or because of its attitude toward black people? Is a book a thing or a gesture, a "being" or a "doing"? Are the laws of literature those of craft or of ideology? Can some alchemy of the intellect reconcile the two? What is the best source of black literature—Western and American civilization, of which black culture is a part, or African civilization, from which black culture has been ripped? What matters more—free sensibility for an elite, or sensible freedom for a race?

The best questions for white readers to ask themselves about black literature are those of fact. They must call a moratorium on their normative judgments. Biases, like rodents on the ropes between ship and pier, run up and down their statements about value. They should also end all but the most tentative kind of descriptive criticism. The ignorance, the failures that make normative criticism arrogant make descriptive criticism inaccurate. The white reader who assumes that he can usefully say whether a black writer is "good" or "bad" is likely to be enough out of touch with present realities to make his analysis of that writer suspect.

Too many white readers, whether they claim to be experts or not, persist in applying the old vocabulary of art to the new forces of black literature. The pricklier writers, like LeRoi Jones, are particularly abused. Only a few critics look directly at Jones, his work, and his concept of black revolutionary cultural nationalism. More people, hiding behind literary traditions, label his work shapeless, chaotic, too mean and too dirty to make sense, or to make his sense acceptable. (One puzzling thing about black literature, of course, is not its homicidal rage, but the lack of it.) Such criticism is actually personal (*Jones scares me but I can't admit that*), political (*Jones is revolutionary and I can't stand for that*), or social (*Jones is unmannerly and I won't stand for that*). The tools of literary criticism thereby become weapons of reprisal, and art itself the victim.

American speech fails to describe our racial agony. Not only is speech untrustworthy because people and institutions have misused it in the past, but its grammatical structure is inadequate. We lack, for example, a pronoun to portray our false collectivity, a *we* to summarize a phony *we-ness*. No vocabulary exists to describe black literature.

Nor do we possess a body of theory, one which is neither adventitious nor malign, that might give order to its contradictions and subtleties and flux. The neglected black critics provided only the beginnings. Black artists are now carrying on with the job. Only blacks can create such a theory. A white attempt to do so, no matter how earnest, will be morally unacceptable. The odds are that it would also be impractical. Besides, a black aesthetic will doubtless explore the relationship between writing and revolutionary politics. Since a common principle of black revolutionary politics is the need for black self-determination, it would be obviously inconsistent for a white person to make critical, authoritative comments.

In the meantime, white Americans should read black literature. They can work to put black writers on reading lists and in libraries. They can support magazines, publishing houses, and theaters which blacks control. Plenty of informed black opinion exists to help white people make intelligent guesses about which black groups serve elements in the black community. White readers must also accept black authority of interpretation. If they speak about black literature, they should speak as informally, as personally, as possible. We have already had enough formal, impersonal white authorities on black literature. And if some of us must teach it (and for deplorable reasons we will probably have to help teach it for a while), the best teaching might well be unorthodox teaching: talk to white students about why they may not always understand, let black students work together if they choose, and never assume that teaching black literature is the road either to salvation or happiness.

For white readers to *like* black writers who threaten them with violence is pathological. Either such readers are masochists who enjoy death warrants; or disbelievers who assume that black writers are simply playing around; or fools who think that the menacing black gesture will never touch them. Yet white readers will find much they might legitimately like. Nearly all black literature emanates an unusual energy. While speaking of murderous times, it proclaims existence. It works with expansive themes: escape, endurance, conflict, the need for dignity, the nature of power. Indeed, it offers white readers the best analysis of white power. Refusing to kowtow to the sacred cows, it dissects the diseases of the American body politic.

Notions of identity are particularly complex in black literature. They are bound up with concepts of freedom; seeking one demands seeking the other; having one means having the other. Much of the writing concerns the agony between the life white people impose upon blacks and a black's private self. Many black characters struggle until the fight consumes them, and they are sacrificed. Many white writers, to be sure, also dramatize the quest for self; but their characters often repudiate the family. For black characters the question of blood is more difficult. Are they black or partly white? If blood is mixed, how should one respond? Like the child of a master class? Like the whelp of rape? Or with indifference? No black character can ignore the family. Many of the best affirm it. So doing, they make family and community, blood and race, near synonyms of speech and feeling. The poet Nikki Giovanni writes, "Black love/is Black Wealth."

Autobiography is a suspect genre. Not only does it subjectively cast doubt on objectivity (even if desirable) about the self and others, but the form itself blurs distinctions between the two: the subject may claim for himself the experience of others. Nor can specific autobiographies be trusted. Some, like those of Booker T. Washington, are crafted to advance public goals: to impress blacks, to please whites, to exemplify black progress, to pledge allegiance to white safety. Yet black autobiographies, including the slave narratives, are unique statements about identity. They appeal because they so little conceal. The black writers, I suspect, are more conscious of their origins and their lives than white writers. As they describe their own lives they also describe a territory and time of history.

Black writing, despite its seriousness, is more than a Literature of Solemnity. Much of it has what Clarence Major calls "radiance." Fantasies, excursions into inner space, are bold and ingenious. Explorations of the supernatural, excursions into cosmic space, are rich and convincing. Wit, both defensive and offensive, is acid and flamboyant. Comedy efficiently exposes individuals and society. A boy, publishing in the journal *What's Happening* and signing himself "Clorox," is on to himself, and others as well.

Black poetry offers complex drama, and intricate new rhythms, syntax and diction. This is Don L. Lee's "We Walk the Way of the New World":

> we run the dangercourse.
> the way of the stocking caps & murray's grease.
> if (u is modern u used duke greaseless hair pomade)
> jo jo was modern/ an international nigger
> 　　　　born: jan. 1, 1863 in new york, mississippi.
> his momma was mo militant than he was/is
> jo jo bes no instant negro
> his development took all of 106 years
> & he was the first to be stamped "made in USA"
> where he arrived bow-legged a curve ahead of the
> 　　20th century's new
> weapon: television.
> which invented, "how to win and influence people"
> and gave jo jo his how/ever look; however u
> 　　want me.
>
> we discovered that with the right brand of cigarettes
> that one, with his best girl,
> cd skip thru grassy fields in living color
> & in slow-motion: Caution: niggers, cigarettes
> 　　smoking
> 　　　　will kill u & yr/health.
> & that the breakfast of champions is: blackeye peas
> 　　& rice.
> & that God is dead & Jesus is black and last seen
> 　　on 63rd street

in a gold & black dashiki, sitting in a pink hog
speaking swahili with a pig-latin accent.
& that integration and coalition are synonymous,
& that the only thing that really mattered was:
who could get the highest on the least or
how to expand & break one's mind.

in the coming world
new prizes are
to be given

we *ran* the dangercourse.
now, it's a silent walk/ a careful eye
jo jo is there
to his mother he is unknown
(she accepted with a newlook: what wd u do if
someone loved u?)
jo jo is back
& he will catch all the new jo jo's as they wander
in & out
and with a fan-like whisper say: you ain't no
tourist
and Harlem ain't for
sight-seeing, brother.[3]

Black plays demand a vital relationship between actors and
audience, which is also participant and chorus. Black novels
promise acute characterization. (In contrast, twentieth-century
white novels tend to cultivate a single sensibility, to lavish
imaginative energy upon the ego in solitude.) Creating characters means not only focusing the imagination upon others,
but also detecting psychological fraud, sniffing out the gap
between illusion and reality, between word and deed: these

[3] "We Walk the Way of the New World" by Don L. Lee, in *Negro
Digest,* September 1969. Reprinted with permission.

gifts exist in abundance in black literature. White American writers often reduce strong women characters to bitches or big-booted, big-boobed, loutish Tugboat Annies. Black writers, if they avoid the temptation to assign outworn sex roles within a rigid nuclear family, give their women characters respect.

Flexible yet structured, like a blues performance, black literature organizes human experience for the sake of experience, vitality and consolation. It reflects a sense of ritual which is both sacred, for addressing the gods, and profane, for addressing the people. In contrast, the official rituals of white America seem metallic. Either they celebrate death (the medal ceremonies in the Rose Garden) or technology (the rocket launchings).

The black writer, himself active, writes books about acts which call for more action; when he does, he is the model of the man of letters. White people, if they read black literature properly, must eventually rebel against their own world, the world which the books reveal: to do nothing but read is to be evasive, to do nothing but speak is to be unspeakable. The end of theory is the call to practice.

The Teaching of Afro-American Literature

BY DARWIN T. TURNER

Darwin Turner, former dean of the Graduate School at North Carolina Agricultural and Technical State University, has edited three anthologies of Afro-American literature and published several articles in the field. He is currently teaching at the University of Michigan. Insisting on the intellectual legitimacy of black literature and describing the past neglect of black authors, Turner feels that this literature is important and vast enough to be integrated into traditional survey courses and taught in separate courses. While recognizing both the emotional and intellectual shortcomings of white scholars, Turner rejects Stimpson's view that only blacks should teach Afro-American literature. Trained scholars, free of racial bias, can teach black literature, he maintains, whatever their color.

ALTHOUGH AFRO-AMERICANS have been writing literature in English since 1746 and publishing books in English since 1773, literature by Afro-Americans has become significantly visible in colleges only within the past several years. As late as 1967 most of the relevant materials were out of print, including the only anthology adequate for a course in Afro-American literature; few, if any, non-black colleges offered courses in Afro-American literature or even studied Afro-American writers, except possibly Richard Wright, James Baldwin, and Ralph Ellison; and scholarly societies and publishers seemed disinterested in studies about black writers. Today, three major anthologies of Afro-American literature are already in print,

Reprinted by permission from *College English* 31, no. 7 (April, 1970): 666–70.

and two more are on the way; at least six publishers—Arno, Atheneum, Negro Universities Press, Mnemosyne Press, the U of Michigan and Collier are frantically reprinting books by and about black writers; courses are burgeoning in predominantly white universities, even in Alabama and Mississippi; and almost any meeting of a professional society in literature will include at least one paper related to Afro-American writers. In truth, the frenzy of attention has elevated Afro-American literature (and Afro-American studies) to a pinnacle recently occupied by atomic physics and new mathematics: It is the exciting new concern of the educational world.

I do not propose to discuss here the nature and scope of Afro-American literature itself. Instead, I wish to consider two controversial issues: 1) the place of Afro-American literature in the curriculum, and 2) criteria for teachers and scholars of Afro-American literature.

I will not spend a lot of time endorsing the academic value of Afro-American literature. Already too much time and breath have been wasted on this issue. Those of us who have sat in meetings of curriculum committees know how seldom the members question the academic value of a proposed course. The committee's most frequent worry is, "How much will it cost?" We also know that some institutions entice a professor to them by guaranteeing that he can "work up" any course he wishes to teach—even one narrowly restricted to a study of Washington Irving, Edgar Allan Poe, and James Fenimore Cooper. Few institutions of prestige question the intellectual content of such courses. (Probably they should; but most do not.)

In a discipline which thus continually reaffirms its assumption that any segment of literary heritage is intellectually valid for study in higher education, it is both absurd and hypocritical to raise the question of academic respectability about the study of the literature of an ethnic group composed of people who have been publishing literary works in America for more than 200 years, who have created some of the best-known folktales in America, and who include among their number such distinguished writers as Jean Toomer, Countee Cullen, Richard Wright, Gwendolyn Brooks, Ralph Ellison, James Baldwin, Lorraine Hansberry, and Le Roi Jones. If anyone has doubts about the respectability of this literature, I urge him merely to read Frederick Douglass's *Narrative of a Slave* or Charles W. Chesnutt's *The Conjure Woman* or Jean Toomer's *Cane* or Robert Hayden's *Selected Poems* or Melvin Tolson's *Rendezvous with America* or *Harlem Gallery* or Margaret Walker's *Jubilee*.

A more significant question to ask is whether these writers should be studied in a separate course or as part of the usual surveys and period courses in American literature. My answer is that they should be studied in both ways.

There is no difficulty about including Afro-American writers in any American literature survey based on aesthetic and thematic criteria. Phillis Wheatley is sometimes praised as the best American neo-classical poet of the 18th century. David Walker's *Appeal* (1828) is as exciting a document as any by Tom Paine. The slave narratives offer interesting parallels with the autobiographies of early white Americans. Any course which wades through James Whitcomb Riley, Thomas Page, and other writers of American dialects can scrutinize Paul Laurence Dunbar. The folktales of Charles Chesnutt furnish intriguing counterpoint to the better known tales of Joel Chandler Harris. James Weldon Johnson's *Autobiography of an Ex-Coloured Man* (1912) compares favorably with the realistic novels of William Dean Howells. Claude McKay's *Home to Harlem* (1928) vividly depicts a segment of that jazzy, lost generation which found other biographers in Ernest

Hemingway and Scott Fitzgerald. In spirit and style Countee Cullen frequently reminds readers of Edna St. Vincent Millay, and Jean Toomer is a logical inclusion in a discussion of the stylistic experiments of Sherwood Anderson and Gertrude Stein. Zora Neale Hurston's *Moses, Man of the Mountain* resembles and perhaps surpasses John Erskine's satires about Helen of Troy and Galahad. And on and on and on. Certainly, if he wishes to, a knowledgeable teacher has no problem fitting Afro-American writers into an American literature survey; for stylistically, black writers often resemble white American authors more closely than they resemble their black contemporaries.

But, for a different reason, Afro-American authors should also be taught in a separate course—not a black "rap" course for revolutionaries, not a watered-down "sop" designed to give three credits to the disadvantaged, but an academically sound course, which may be even more valuable for white students than for black. The reason for such a course is educational or —if you wish—political. Before protesting that our concern is artistic literature not politics, let us remind ourselves that college teachers do teach those documents at the beginnings of most anthologies of American literature—the writings of John Smith and Cotton Mather, the Mayflower Compact, etc. Let us remember also the courses in New England Writers and Southern Regional Writers. The documents provide a student with awareness of the intellectual and social history of America; the regional courses help him to understand the styles and attitudes of writers who represent a selected population in America. For similar reasons, courses in literature by Afro-American writers must be taught.

As we all know, in a two-term survey of American literature we cannot include all the writers who deserve to be taught: some worthy writers must be omitted. A concerned teacher consoles himself that a student's intellectual growth is not seriously impaired by lack of knowledge of the writers omitted; for, at some point between the first grade and the sixteenth, a student will probably read most of the writers omitted from the survey. Or if he does not read those specific writers, he reads others who offer comparable styles and attitudes: Bret Harte or Mark Twain rather than Riley, Stephen Crane or Edith Wharton rather than Howells, Ernest Hemingway or Edgar Lee Masters rather than Gertrude Stein. Thus, a student learns that literary excellence can be discovered in all regions of America and in all periods of American history. If no writer is included who can be identified as Hungarian or Italian or Polish, neither the teacher nor the student is alarmed; for, in other courses, the student has already learned that intellectual and artistic masterpieces have been produced in all of the countries of Europe.

One cannot, however, regard with such complacency the omission of Afro-American writers from the survey; for in sixteen years of schooling, a student will probably never read these writers in any other course except a course about Afro-American writers. As I have stated, the reason for concern is not merely an aesthetic issue of whether a student may miss an opportunity for pleasure or art that a black writer may provide. Even more important is the fact that the student lives in a society which, for more than three hundred years, has denigrated the intellectual and cultural capability of black Africans and their descendants. The student has been taught this doctrine of inferiority in books and lectures prepared by respectable professors, in newspapers and magazines, in motion pictures and theater, and even in the church and his home. The only way to repudiate this myth of inferiority is to amass as much evidence to the contrary as possible. But the evidence cannot rest upon two or three black writers since 1940 or

1950: Richard Wright, James Baldwin, and Ralph Ellison, for example. Too easily these few are adjudged the exceptions or are used to exemplify a second myth—that Afro-Americans have developed respectable culture only within the past twenty-five years. The requisite education must study *many* black writers from the eighteenth century to the present—not in a chauvinistic glorification of their effort but in a critical examination of their literary and intellectual merits in relation to the standards, customs, interest, and knowledge which characterized the periods during which they wrote.

A second controversial issue concerns the criteria for selecting a teacher. Conventionally, a teacher's competence to offer a course is determined from evidence of his study and publication in the area. But a serious question has been raised about the competence of a white teacher to teach literature by black writers. Few people of academic background deny that white teachers can learn to teach black literature, just as black teachers can teach white literature. And they realize that, if all colleges were to establish courses in Afro-American literature, the number of courses alone would necessitate the use of white teachers. Nevertheless, many black educators continue to worry that some white teachers will teach the course so badly that they will create more harm than good. Frequently, a black teacher who makes such a statement is accused of racist thinking. Perhaps the accusers are remembering with guilt the fact that, until recently, most white administrators and faculties made little effort to hire qualified black scholars to teach courses in English and American literature. But the black who objects to white teachers is not merely prejudiced; he sees weaknesses which the white teacher must overcome if he wishes to teach Afro-American literature well.

First, some white teachers will teach the course badly because, ignorant of the complexity of the subject matter, they will not take the time to prepare themselves adequately. In the English departments of most universities, a teacher is entrusted with the responsibility for an advanced course, such as one in American Romantics or Victorian Prose, only after years of preparation. In several years of college, he studies the works, critical commentaries about the works, the lives of the authors, and the historical culture in which the works were produced. He not only listens to lectures and reads assigned works; he even conducts independent research in the materials. After such preparation, he is finally permitted to teach a traditional course. In contrast, a teacher may be thrust into a course in Afro-American literature after formal preparation of a summer or even less.

Furthermore, the average white teacher is handicapped by the fact that he has not had the informal or extra-disciplinary experiences which might familiarize him with the material. Consider, in contrast, the manner in which the black teacher of American literature, let us say, is provided, outside the English classroom, with awareness of the materials about which white Americans are writing. He has been forced to read many, many books of history about white Americans; he cannot read a newspaper or magazine without reading factual as well as propagandistic articles about their attitudes, desires, virtues, vices, and living habits. He sees them advertised on the motion picture screen, on television, on billboards. In short, wherever he turns—even within the black community— he is learning about white Americans. The average *white* American, however, has probably known few black people intimately, has read few books by black writers, and until recently has read few presentations about black Americans (and those few have concentrated on the "problem" which the black man poses for America or for himself). Putting it simply, the average white teacher is ignorant about black people and does not even know where to turn for reliable information about such basic matters as the meanings of slang used by blacks, the traditional jokes, and the popular stereotypes of heroes and villains. This individual will teach Afro-American literature ineptly until he learns what he needs to know.

A second failing of the well-intentioned teacher is that, subconsciously, he may be a racist. That is, subconsciously, he may believe that black people actually are innately inferior or that historically they have been made inferior by society. This attitude may cause him to bungle the course in either of two different ways. One, believing that a black writer cannot produce literary work of a quality which would be required of a white writer, the teacher may praise trash because he does not expect anything better from a black writer. Such unconscious patronizing insults black writers. Or, two, a well-meaning humanitarian may become paternalistic. Believing himself securely established in American society and, therefore, superior in judgment to those who are not, he may condemn the philosophy of life which the black author proposes for himself. A teacher has the right to assert that any writer—black or white—has failed to clarify his ideas or has failed to develop them effectively, but only a pompous paternalist will insist that he is better qualified than the writer to determine what the writer should have thought about himself, his race, and his relation to other people. I wish that I were exaggerating these failings, but one sees them too frequently in articles currently published about Afro-American literature.

A third well-intentioned teacher who fails is the one who becomes excessively sentimental about the problems which black people experience in a white-oriented society. Such a teacher may wail about the problems in a frenzy which sickens black students who have learned that tears offer escape not solutions.

These three types of teachers—the unprepared, the subconscious racist, the sentimentalist—can be pitied for their failure. A fourth cannot be. He is the individual who views Afro-American literature as a vehicle for rapid promotion. He is the "instant expert," striving solely for grants and publications.

A final problem for the white teacher is not directly of his own making. Even if he *has* prepared conscientiously, black students may distrust him because their years of living in America have taught them to distrust white men's attitudes towards black culture. They will be looking for the teacher who makes the mistake, if he selects autobiography, of choosing *Manchild in the Promised Land* rather than *The Autobiography of Malcolm X*. They will be waiting for the teacher who does not understand the slang of the black community. In short, they will be looking for the racist or the fool hidden behind a mask. And a lot of valuable course time can be lost while the teacher proves himself to his students.

The white teacher of Afro-American literature must recognize and anticipate these problems and potential failings. But do not let my castigation of white teachers promote false assumptions about the ability of blacks. A black or brown face is not in itself sufficient qualification for teaching Afro-American literature. True, a black man is generally more sensitive to the language, attitudes, and nuances of the black writer; he has the informal, extra-disciplinary knowledge of the subject matter of the writers. But he too must study sufficiently to know Afro-American literature in its historical development, and he must be competent to teach literature.

Literature by Afro-Americans is a new, exciting subject matter for curricula. It needs to be taught, but only by teachers—black or white—who do all the homework which is required.

Black History in the College Curriculum

BY JOANNA E. SCHNEIDER AND
ROBERT L. ZANGRANDO

Joanna E. Schneider, formerly a legislative assistant in the U.S. Office of Education, is a candidate for the Ph.D. in American Studies at George Washington University. Robert L. Zangrando, formerly assistant executive secretary of the American Historical Association, is history and social science editor at Yale University Press and a lecturer in history at Yale. Schneider and Zangrando agree with several other contributors to this volume that there should be greater focus in the universities on the role of blacks in American history. They call for a novel approach in this area: lower standards for hiring black teachers and separate classes for black and white students, with black teachers conducting the former and whites conducting the latter.

BLACK PROTEST cannot be contained. Because it stems from a long and bitter realization of basic injustices throughout every aspect of American society, and because it rests on both an intellectual and an emotional awareness of these injustices, Black protest will grow and remain a vibrant force for change for many years to come. The academic community cannot escape its impact, nor should it wish to do so. Indeed, Black protest in the nation's universities, colleges, and public schools might well prove to be the most singularly important influence on the substance and nature of education in this century.

Working with concerned elements of the white liberal com-

Reprinted by permission from *The Rocky Mountain Social Science Journal* VI (October, 1969): 134–42.

munity, Negro protest leaders during the first two-thirds of this century have laid the foundations for a major social revolution in race relations. At all levels throughout public and private institutional networks, Negro spokesmen have successfully pressed for legislation, judicial decisions, executive orders, and privately initiated actions that have given Black people, at least in theory, the opportunities to enter fully into the American system. But such public and private actions have often represented a statement of intent on the part of the white community rather than a guarantee of performance. Consequently, Black protest has intensified, and Black spokesmen have sought in new and imaginative ways to wrest from a reluctant society the same daily privileges whites enjoy. One of the most precious and necessary of these privileges is the opportunity to confront, to examine, and to interpret the past. In the final analysis, this is what Black history is all about.

The time had to come when Black protest would turn its anger upon the academic community, when Black spokesmen would turn their fire not merely upon the white man's performance but, more importantly, upon his entire intellectual and emotional perspective. In doing so, Black Americans have declared that self-awareness on the race issue is crucial for white and Black men alike, and that a healthy self-awareness cannot possibly be achieved without a correction of the distortions, omissions, and fallacies that have so often marked traditional historical scholarship dealing with race in the American past. In demanding the reassessment of the past, Black spokesmen have sought to widen and enrich the nation's historical perspective, for Black history blends the vital elements of reform: intellectual honesty, Black identity, white awareness, the transmission of knowledge, and the exercise of power based upon that knowledge. Scholars and non-academicians alike should welcome and encourage the thrust for Black history and Black studies, whatever may be their fears about the difficulties and disruptive changes that will necessarily mark the academic community during the transitional, implemental period.

In recent years, the American academic community has increasingly recognized that, for the most part, those engaged in historical research and history instruction have failed to confront the realities of race. Black men and women have not been accorded their proper places in the recounting of the nation's past, and surely the attitudes, motivations, and conduct of white Americans in the matter of race relations have not been accurately reported. While it is true that many colleges and universities have recently instituted courses in Black history and Black studies, these efforts have often been made for the wrong reasons. Not infrequently, such courses have been insufficiently conceived and supported, and they have been undertaken without a full awareness of Black history's solid educational potential. Even where shortcomings are not apparent, faculty and students alike must continually assess ongoing courses to be sure that emergent and newly visible needs are met. The successful development of a viable Black history program involves questions of curriculum, staff, materials and resources, methodologies, and overall concepts and objectives. These deserve some brief comment.

To begin with, a course or an entire program in Black history must be designed and implemented on the clear understanding that it does represent a departure from tradition; flexibility, innovation, change, and initiative must mark the effort. Much of the criticism against Black history has stemmed from the failure of its critics fully to appreciate this need for flexibility and innovation. To begin with, the thrust for Black history can profit directly from the enthusiasm and pressures generated by Black militant students and some of their collaborative white peers. At a time when it is clearly evident that American higher education is under attack by students, and when it has become increasingly apparent that students respond to the traditional courses and curriculums with apathy, indifference, and anger, Black history finds itself almost unique in that it represents a link between historical scholarship and student interest. Administrators and educators should willingly capitalize on this powerful motivational factor. It is true, of course, that these very pressures sometimes take the form of demands for Black history taught only by Black professors to Black students alone. Instead of viewing these as unreasonable demands, or ones that seem to violate recent liberal integrationist tradition, college administrators and educators should devise ways to employ such pressures for the benefit of curricular change. If they fail to do so, they will have abdicated their responsibilities to Black and white students alike.

What is to prevent institutions of higher education from constructing parallel courses open to Black and white students at the option of each? Whether or not we like to admit it, the nature of racism in the United States—in both its historic and its contemporary aspects—has exposed the Black man to experiences that are different in type and degree from those of his white counterpart. There is good justification for arguing that only Black people can fully understand the historic dimensions of racism and of the Black experience in America. This justification does not stem from racial differences in biological terms; rather, it is the consequence of different environmental experiences imposed on the Black man by the white community. Social scientists have never been reluctant to rely upon experience and empirical evidence in teaching economic, political, and social history. They should be equally open to instructional experimentation based on the experiences and empirical knowledge of Black students and instructors. If there were a dual system, Black and white students would be free to take parallel courses in Black history in ways which conceivably could maximize learning and motivational involvement for all parties. Options that would allow students to shift from section to section within a parallel course system may offend college registrars, but if the results we seek are educational in nature, bureaucratic fears cannot be permitted to forestall experimentation.

In terms of flexibility, it will also be necessary for administrators and faculty members to be less rigid about the standards of training they have customarily applied in hiring instructional staff. There is no point in denying that this nation and its institutions of higher learning have done a very poor job of preparing Black people to fill leadership roles for the society at large or for the Black community itself. It seems fairly hypocritical, with that background of failure, for white administrators now to impede the teaching of Black history to Black men on grounds that these prospective faculty members do not fit the "standards" long accepted in white educational circles. The value of having Black people teach Black history stems from the fact that, because of the experiences that have been theirs in this society, they will readily bring different perspectives, new orientations, and different questions to an examination of historical evidence. And since the strength of historical investigation rests on the quality and diversity of the questions asked of the data, the infusion of a whole range of new questions and new perspectives offers history, as a discipline, an unprecedented opportunity for growth and development. This will be a major legacy of Black history, if white educators are perceptive enough to understand the potential.

Given the will and the investment of sufficient resources, there is no doubt that the educational community can develop, over time, the number of highly competent, professionally trained Black historians that will be needed. But, during an interim period, we must be willing to support, work with, and welcome Black instructors and scholars who do not seem immediately to meet long established and too-little-questioned "standards" of academic preparation. It would be tempting for some traditionalists to argue that offerings in Black history must wait upon the day when a sufficiently large cadre of Black instructors is prepared and ready to take its "full" place in the ranks of college instructors. Such an argument can hardly carry weight and conviction in light of the crisis—educational and societal—that we face. Moreover, such a position ignores the fact that American higher education has repeatedly faced scarcities of "competent" personnel, but it has made the necessary adjustments. These adjustments have always meant a bountiful infusion of resources and an unquestioned commitment to develop competent staff over time. Hand-in-hand with that has gone an acceptance of new personnel and innovative techniques in instruction during an interim period. Why should the case be any different for Black history? Why should American higher education not accept the same types of commitments, generate the same sorts of enthusiasms, invest comparable amounts of resources and energies, and profit equally from the effort? Certainly American higher education has never been averse to doing just this over the past century. During the last third of the nineteenth century (building upon the Morrill Act of 1862), this society developed the phenomenon of the land-grant institution committed to the concept that publicly supported institutions of higher education had a responsibility to design curriculums and programs specifically to meet the needs of an agricultural and an increasingly industrialized society. The agricultural extension programs of the late 1880's reflected this willingness to put institutions of higher education at the disposal of the community; so, too, did college and university programs in home economics and vocational education during the twentieth century. And, more recently, the National Science Foundation, the National Defense Education Act, and the National Endowment for the Arts and Humanities have all indicated America's willingness to expand its investments in higher education for the purpose of meeting contemporary public needs. Such readily available historical models counter the objections of those who seem hesitant to employ resources on behalf of Black history and Black studies programs.

Since the introduction of Black history courses and programs does represent an important substantive—not procedural—departure for American higher education, there will be a period in the years ahead during which we will all be experimenting and feeling our way. In an age when student protest reflects a disenchantment with decisions made at a distance from the classroom by faceless college administrators, what better opportunity to mobilize and employ student willingness to participate in curricular changes and instructional programs than to invest students—particularly Black students —with a hand in structuring and conducting Black history courses? Everything we know about learning theory and the extent to which the active participant is a demonstrably more effective learner argues for this as well.

Undoubtedly there are many white faculty members who feel threatened by pressures for Black history taught only by Black instructors. In human terms this is a perfectly understandable concern; in light of the realities of racism in America, it may also be a concern stemming—even if unconsciously —from white biases. Taking these in reverse order, there seems to be little that can be done immediately about white prejudice. But there is much that can be done about institutional networks and academic ground rules that will temper white professional fears. Those white instructors who fear displacement might rest more easily if faculty groups and administrators were to develop parallel courses that could utilize white talents to the fullest. After all, there are now and there will remain millions of white students who need to learn Black history. There will be no decline in the enormity of this task; the challenge is rather to fashion opportunities for white faculty members who want to work in Black history to do so productively, together with those white and Black students who decide to study with them. The strengths and competencies that white instructors do have might be incorporated into team-teaching situations with Black professors. This will not always be an optimal solution, but it is one possible alternative for students and faculty who wish to capitalize on the resources that are at hand. Long after our initial efforts have been expended, new opportunities and needs—to be met with further imagination and initiative—will become apparent. The process will be an open-ended and evolving one.

The development of effective and meaningful courses in Black history will not be easily accomplished. It is one thing mechanically to introduce another course into the catalog or into a department's offerings. If that should be the depth of the effort, it will prove an academic failure and it will further antagonize and disrupt human relations on campus. The challenge, and the exciting possibility, seems rather from a unique chance for this generation of scholars and students to shape a fresh approach to an important area of historical studies that has thus far received too little attention.

Recently there has been a steady production of monographic studies and documentary volumes in Black history. In the years that lie ahead, this ambitious beginning will prove, in retrospect, but a meager start. Scholarly articles, books, major biographies, penetrating case studies, and interpretative syntheses will continue to appear for use in Black history courses. There will be, in other words, no lack of resources as historians have traditionally defined them. But the existing prospect in the case of Black history rests equally with the types of materials that have been too little utilized—in fact too little recognized—in classroom experiences. There exists throughout the Black community an endless wealth of untapped resources. These will be found within the network of Black community life: Black churches, Black political institutions and organizations, Black protest movements, Black businesses, and the vibrant but often discounted world of extra-legal activities that represent, in part, the Black man's accommodation to and survival within a larger white society. Ways of uncovering, identifying, and employing such resources for both research and instructional purposes in higher education will require initiative far beyond that which has customarily characterized the standard approach of American educators. Three decades ago those who pioneered the development of American studies and American civilization programs developed multidisciplinary and innovative techniques for confronting and utilizing elements of popular and material culture. While these have sometimes been regarded as unwelcome departures by historical traditionalists, such efforts have undoubtedly enriched our understanding of the American past. A similar type of experimentation is necessary for a multifaceted approach to Black history, if the task is to be carried out in productive and scholarly terms.

We shall have to continue our customary research techniques and data-gathering through an examination of archival sources, personal and private collections of letters, public records and documents, and the like. But largely because white America has never recognized the legitimacy of Black culture and has either ignored or misunderstood the institutional network within the Black community, white scholars have overlooked many of the resources—written, oral, and material—extant within Black America. With proper funding from public and private agencies, these materials can be gathered, cataloged, and made readily accessible for research and instructional purposes by Black and white students alike. Moreover, it is precisely in this crucial area of data-gathering among sources hitherto neglected that Black scholars, students, and researchers can play a notably productive role.

Central to these methodological innovations in both instruction and research are the questions that instructors and students must raise about Black history: questions about values, social relationships over time, the economic and political implications of the Black experience, the nature of racism, the psychic and socio-psychic role of a repressed minority in a growing and affluent society, the variants of protest, and the nature of repression and retaliation. Too few of these aspects of the Black experience in America have been explored; even fewer of them have been approached in a multidisciplinary sense; all of them await a fresh perspective built upon a quality of inquiry seldom brought to the study of the Black experience. It is yet too early to predict what the nature of all these questions can and will be. But the great promise of extensive work in Black history, by Blacks and whites alike, is that it will move the entire historical profession—instructors and students, learners of all sorts—to new, different, and (one assumes) higher levels of expectation and performance than we have yet attained in either Black history or United States history generally. The challenge is enormous and the potential still beyond the horizon in its full realization.

Much of what we have said thus far touches on the objectives, short-range and long-range, of Black historical studies.

But there are certain points that must be stated more explicitly.

To begin with, a normally confident, occasionally smug and self-righteous, society that has seldom been tested beyond its means has not yet begun to ask appropriate questions about what it means for a repressed minority, Black Americans, to have survived three-and-a-half centuries within its midst. In an age of potential thermonuclear destruction or of protracted attrition, born of an endless series of limited foreign wars and unresolved domestic conflicts, basic questions of survival and community operation under stress and tension deserve high priority as topics for thorough study. Today's Black community and its predecessors understand survival far better than most white Americans can. It is precisely for this reason that new questions about phenomena of conflict resolution and survival in the contemporary world, and in the past, need to be pursued.

We are just now beginning to probe the extent of racism in this society. An examination of this from a multidisciplinary perspective, within an historical framework, will make a considerable difference in our understanding about the problems of today and the dilemmas of the past. This holds true not only for Black history, but also for an honest appraisal of the American past in terms of how the dominant white majority came to grips with the presence of Black, Red, and Yellow men. Unless we can fully comprehend the role of racism in this society, we shall never truly know America. Black history offers us an indispensable opportunity to do so.

Since the early seventeenth century, Americans have held certain comfortable assumptions about their own goodness and potential perfectability. To a degree, this was laudable for a people who wished consciously to build a better society. Woven into these assumptions were beliefs about the value of individualism and the role of individuals participating equally in community decisions that fashioned their destiny. We know that these assumptions were too seldom fulfilled in practice. Colonial settlers were strongly biased against colonists of other religions, settlers from other nations, and members of their own community of different socioeconomic ranks; moreover, they were suspicious and contemptuous of non-whites. Americans have, in a sense, built a nation upon the deception that they are a community of co-equal individuals participating co-equally in community affairs. Solid studies in Black history will put that illusion into perspective. And if the psychic health of an individual is grounded upon a truthful self-awareness, that same type of honesty is no less essential for a community or society. A multidisciplinary approach to Black history will necessarily have to come to grips with questions of the individual's role in society, the degree of autonomy with which individuals have functioned in the American past, and the extent of power or powerlessness that individuals or groups have had in our national experience. Black history can give the American society unparalleled insights into the deficiencies of its own value system as carried out in practice. Black history has been justified on the grounds that it will give a new and fresh sense of identity to Black people. This is undoubtedly so, but it is equally true that the same fresh sense of perspective can also be gained for members of the dominant white majority from a study of Black history. Finally, Black history is relevant. By examining authentic problems that touch both the present and the past, Black history joins student motivation and historical reality. These two are essential ingredients for effective learning.

Those who would teach and do research in Black history face no small task. If done properly, that task could help revolutionize the entire society. If we are mature and honest enough to confront both the challenge and opportunities, this revolution need not be violent and destructive. Rather, in the best sense of new knowledge—however painful—it could be a thoroughly rejuvenating and cathartic experience for a troubled nation. If open-endedness and the spirit of innovation are present, and if college and university administrators, faculty members, and students are willing to invest the necessary resources, support, and patience, then the role of Black history in higher education can be exceedingly productive and therapeutic. Universities are designed to encourage learning and to create an atmosphere for inquiry. Pragmatic Americans have repeatedly utilized the resources of their universities in meeting crucial public needs. Black history fits into the best traditions of higher learning, while at the same time it offers an unprecedented chance to alter university programs and, even, the society at large. It would be foolish to hope for immediate and broadcast results. It would be delusive to think that a great number of false starts and frustrations do not lie before us. It would be shortsighted to assume that any models we might develop would be finished products needing no further change and refinement. But if we are willing to accept the hazards and benefits, ready to expose ourselves to unknown consequences, and able to adjust to unanticipated results, then Black history will become a major force for historical truth and a major step toward strengthening and invigorating the historical profession, revitalizing higher education, and saving this troubled society from itself.

Black Studies
and the Role
of the Historian

BY JOHN W. BLASSINGAME

Blassingame calls on historians, black and white, to study the black past dispassionately. White historians, foundations, and publishers, he declares, must accept responsibility for oppressing Negro historians and for consciously defending white supremacy by writing and publishing racist tracts which passed for historical studies. He argues, however, that the kind of training white historians received and the milieu in which they worked were probably as important as racism for the kind of history they wrote. While he believes that black scholars must challenge the white supremacist tenets underlying American history, he cautions against the creation of new myths. Blacks, he contends, need a realistic assessment of their past if they are to have any hope of improving their contemporary situation. Blassingame also believes that color cannot be used as the standard in choosing teachers and expresses the fear that the application of this standard in Black Studies will cause Negroes to be barred from teaching white-oriented subjects. He asserts that white historians have generally written about Negroes in order to increase their understanding of white men and white institutions while Negro historians have written about the victories, defeats, hopes, aspirations, ideas, and actions of black men. It is impossible to determine who has written most of the "significant" works.

THE GUNS AT CORNELL and the bombs at San Francisco State College a few years ago made all of us painfully aware of the emotionalism which characterizes the black studies debate. One of the most emotional issues involved in the debate

This is a revised version of a paper delivered December 28, 1969, at the American Historical Association meeting in Washington, D.C.

is the nature of history as it is related to black people. As a student of history, my stake in the resolution of this debate is so large that I am compelled to try to analyze, as dispassionately as possible, the conflicting views, the ambiguities, the dangers, and the prospects it involves.

Blacks have charged, and rightfully so, that American historians have either willfully distorted or ignored the role the Negro has played in American history. The black students are vehemently denouncing the so-called moral-neutrality approach of American historians to race relations. They see clearly that it was not a neutral approach. Instead, historians hid their offensive against the black man, their defense of the status quo, and their battle to preserve white supremacy behind allegations of neutrality. As a result, blacks view white historians as intellectual lynchers, ku kluxers, and whitecappers. Carter G. Woodson expressed this attitude in 1931 when he observed that "to handicap a student for life by teaching him that his black face is a curse and that his struggle to change his condition is hopeless is the worst kind of lynching."

Because they have been lynched and castrated so long by white historians, blacks are now demanding redress. The black students are repeating, in strident tones, the lament of Jean Christophe, "If we had something we could show you, if we had something we could show ourselves, you would respect us and we might respect ourselves. If we had even the names of our great men! If we could lay our hands on things we've made, monuments and towers and palaces, we might find our strength. . . ."

The sins of omission and commission represent a fearful indictment of the historical profession. The black historian Edward A. Johnson demonstrated the impact of this on Negroes when he wrote in 1890:

I have often observed the sin of omission and commission on the part of white authors, most of whom seem to have written exclusively for white children, and studiously left out the many creditable deeds of the Negro. The general tone of most of the histories taught in our schools has been that of the inferiority of the Negro, whether actually said in so many words, or left to be implied from the highest laudation of the deeds of one race to the complete exclusion of those of the other. It must, indeed, be a stimulus to any people to be able to refer to their ancestors as distinguished in deeds of valor, and peculiarly so to the colored people. But how must the little colored child feel when he has completed the assigned course of U.S. History and in it found not one word of credit, not one word of favorable comment for even one among the millions of his foreparents who have lived through nearly three centuries of his country's history! The Negro is hardly given a passing notice in many of the histories taught in the schools; he is credited with no heritage of valor; he is mentioned only as a slave. . . .

As the black student reviews the record of our historical associations, he sees nothing which would indicate the probability of fair treatment of the Negro in our writings. Before 1954 there were few papers on the Negro read at our annual meetings and black scholars reading or commenting on them were even rarer. The profession has generally ignored the Negro's friends and rewarded his enemies. It has frequently honored Phillips and Coulter while generally refusing to elect Du Bois, Woodson, Charles Wesley, Rayford Logan, or Earle Thorpe to honorific posts.

The barriers raised by white scholars, publishers, and foundations against the Negro are primarily responsible for the contemporary shortage of black scholars. Generally it was the settled policy of the foundations to withhold support from those black scholars who would not dance to their tunes. According to Du Bois, this was the fate of Carter Woodson: "Only those persons who followed the [Booker] Washington philosophy . . . could be sure to have encouragement and help. After a while it became the settled policy of philanthropic foundations and of academic circles to intimate that Carter Woodson was altogether too self-centered and self-assertive to receive any great encouragement."

The discriminatory practices of the foundations are revealed clearly in the historical research they have supported. They have, for instance, enthusiastically supported such projects as "Architectural Designs of Bridges in New York, 1840–45, and What They Reveal About American Life" and "Graffiti on Ancient Ruins as an Index of Greek Thought." Yet, they generally refused to support Du Bois or Woodson's efforts to compile a multi-volumed Encyclopedia of the Negro.

Few people understand the burden the Negro scholar has borne. Largely debarred from first-rate graduate schools, or granted a "Negro degree" after he was admitted, the black scholar was informed by his professors that the black past was not worth examining. There was no respite for the Negro scholar. Graduation only raised him to a new level of pain. If he tried to keep up with current research by attending professional meetings, white scholars insulted him, denied him accommodations, or told him that "niggers aren't allowed here." If he sought to utilize the skills he had gained in investigating the black past, white scholars barred him from public libraries, state and historical society archives, and the libraries of predominantly white colleges. If he somehow managed to write a book or an article, he found a "for whites only" sign over the printing presses. Yet, he struggled on, overworked and underpaid, only to die ignominiously—unmourned by the black students he sought to teach and mocked by an America he sought to enlighten.

The racism of American historians is directly responsible for the contemporary attitudes of blacks toward history. Black activists, for example, have created the myth of the heroic, rebellious, militant Negro to counter the white man's myth of Sambo, the obsequious half-man, half-child. White racism has been so pervasive and history so distorted, some of the students argue, that blacks can only improve their self-image by telling bigger lies than white historians told in the past. According to the students, the white historian has shown that he cannot study, write, or teach about blacks objectively. Historically, blacks have questioned whether it is possible for oppressed groups to receive fair treatment intellectually at the hands of their oppressors. In 1841 an anonymous contributor to the *Colored American* argued that "The oppressed are ever their best representatives. Their short and even abrupt expression of intense feeling, is more effectual than the most refined and polished eloquence, prompted though it be, by deep humanity and strong human-heartedness."

Many of the black students have rejected white scholars because they realize that, unlike black historians, many whites have only a temporary interest in Afro-American history because it is currently fashionable. All too many whites view the subject as a new fad; they are studying it because of the fantastic profits to be made. A number of those who rushed forward as "authorities" a few years ago have already made their killing and gone on to teach other subjects. Consequently, the black students contend that it is better, in the long run, to hire black teachers because they are more committed to black history and more likely to have a life-long interest in the subject. It is also obvious to many of them that if they do not reject white historians, the more racist colleges (especially those in the South) will use all kinds of subterfuges to keep from hiring any blacks.

Since a subjective experience can only be understood by those who have undergone it, the white historian, the students contend, is inherently incapable of understanding the black experience. Those blacks who subscribe to this view are convinced that only black historians should write about the black experience. These ideas are not new; they have been expressed by blacks, in one form or another, throughout American history. For example, in 1827 John B. Russwurm asserted in the first issue of *Freedom's Journal,* "We wish to plead for our cause. Too long have others spoken for us. Too long has the public been deceived by misrepresentations, in things which concern us dearly." The black historian G. P. Hamilton expressed similar views 70 years ago:

> No people can be sure of impartial history if the narrators of their history are members of a different race, with views and traditions that are diametrically opposite and often inimical to the interests and welfare of those whose history they write. Impartial history can be written only by unprejudiced minds, for even the scales of justice tremble in the presence of bias and unnecessary hatred. The tendency from many outside sources has ever been to belittle the history of the Negro race and to deny that the race has ever done aught that is worthy of narrating. . . . The only remedy for the race is to produce its own narrators and historians to perpetuate the deeds that reflect honor and glory on it.

It is clearly obvious to most blacks that the profession has done little to promote "impartial" history since Hamilton wrote those words. The black students, therefore, endorse the views of the black poet, Otis Shackleford, that "We must have poets to sing of our deeds and we must have historians to record them . . . We are left alone to tell our tales of woe and to sing our songs of gladness."

Historians have reacted in various ways to the charges of the black students. Historians have been practically unanimous in their alarm over the new myths demanded by many blacks. They have lamented the possibility that these myths will stir up racial hatred. In spite of the apparently straightforward call for truth, there are many contradictions in the arguments of historians of this stripe.

The black revolutionary, it seems to me, has adequate precedents for using history to build pride. We all know that Clio has not retained her virtue intact over the centuries. However regrettable it may be, history has been used by nationalist and ethnic groups through the ages to satisfy their emotional need for pride, for heroes. In truth, the nationalist, the revolutionary, the racist has never demanded objective history; if genuine heroes are not found, he creates his own. Ron Karenga, therefore, is only paraphrasing his white revolutionary predecessors when he writes: "In terms of history, all we need at this point is heroic images; the white boy got enough dates for everybody. . . . Blacks must be their own historians and develop their own heroic images and heroic deeds."

The alarmists have certainly misread the impact of propaganda on the black masses. The most objective catalogue of America's treatment of blacks, Indians, and Orientals will engender indignation, anger, and hatred in the oppressed groups and guilt in the oppressor. I believe that this is good if the anger is translated into incessant demands for justice by the oppressed and the guilt leads to a determination to be just by the oppressor. The claim that the propagandist is stirring up this hatred, however, gives him too much credit. To a black man consigned to the dunghill of American society, history can give him little more reason to hate white America than he already has. Contemporary black hatred of whites has nothing at all to do with Crispus Attucks. Rather, it is a result of the daily oppression which confronts the black man *now*.

The greatest confusion over this issue has developed as a result of the white historian's blanket condemnation of his black colleagues. These arguments are similar, in many ways, to views frequently expressed during the days when the white racist reigned supreme in the historical profession. At that time, most studies by blacks were greeted with scorn by whites, rarely reviewed, and treated merely as propaganda. These are the historians described by Nathan Hare as: "the ultra 'objective' who, though they think nothing of teaching a 'regular' history course without ever mentioning 'the Negro' except as a slave and a spark for the Civil War, are quick to wail self-righteously that to teach from a black perspective is political rather than academic." The current lamentations about the trend toward a black version of history, naturally false, and a white version, naturally true, betray an alarming degree of ignorance about the direction of American historiography. Many contemporary white historians have reached a more objective view of the American past because Woodson, Quarles, Du Bois, Logan, Franklin, and A. A. Taylor raised revolutionary challenges to their theories years ago. Is it not possible that the same thing will be true 30 years from now in regard to the writings of Sterling Stuckey, Lerone Bennett, and Vincent Harding?

Overwhelmed by guilt, most white historians have made only feeble efforts to answer the charge of racism leveled at the profession. This contention, while true, must be placed in perspective. Since he lived in an overwhelmingly racist society, the white historian was severely limited in the past in his ability to be objective when writing about blacks. Constantly subjected to racist ideas, blatant or subtle, in his family, school, church, newspaper, radio, and television, almost inevitably he developed a psychological stake in preserving white supremacy. He shared, for example, white America's fear of black men so completely that he could not even discuss the historical fact of sexual relations between black men and white women. Because his contemporaries rejected the possibility of any Negro achieving anything, in his writings about mixed bloods and famous Negroes he either co-opted them for the white race or when Negroes deviated from the popular stereotype he described them as "atypical." In this strange caricature of history, Benjamin Franklin and Thomas Jefferson were "representative Americans," but Norbert Rillieux, Patrick Healy, Frederick Douglass and other famous black men could not be "representative Negroes."

Until recently, there were few white Americans who were willing to accept the truth about black-white relations. The American white man had such a great capacity to delude himself that the truth about himself was not credible. This, for instance, lies at the heart of our endless debates about the nature of slavery. Because they were writing and reading about their own white fathers, few whites were able to accept the cruelty that was inherent in slavery. To do so was to reveal how similar their own ideas were to those of slaveholders and, more importantly, how degraded a white man could become in his relations with blacks.

The real reason for the distortion of the role of blacks in our history is probably related as much to the nature of the historian's task as to racism. The problem is twofold in nature. First of all, American historians were so woefully ill-trained in the past that they were not equipped to study Negro history systematically. Second, the Negro became the "invisible man" of American history largely because he left few literary sources and because American historians were not trained to use other kinds of sources. Essentially, the Negro has been left out of our history for the same reason that all largely illiterate or non-English speaking groups have been left out of it. Upper-class, generally racist whites wrote and published an over-whelming majority of the books, newspapers, magazines, letters, and diaries the historian uses. Far too many of our glimpses of the Negro are filtered through the eyes of racist whites or distorted by them through their control of the presses. When the black poet James D. Corrothers submitted an article describing the progress of the black community in Chicago to the *Chicago Tribune,* for example, a white reporter rewrote it, deleting all of the material about Negro progress and putting dialect in the mouths of Negroes who spoke En-glish perfectly.

Since Indians, blacks, the poor, laborers, and Orientals left few records, the harried historian, when dealing with these groups, has the almost impossible task of describing a debate when only one debater has recorded his views. We face, then, Anatole France's classic formulation of the historian's di-lemma, "We have never heard the devil's side of the story: God wrote all the books." Given the bias inherent in literary sources, the paucity of records left by Negroes, and the gaps in the training of most American historians, the surprising thing is not the way white historians have written about blacks, but that they wrote about them at all. Considering all of the factors listed above, it is clear that an overwhelming majority of the white historians should never have tried to write about blacks.

Most of the whites who wrote about blacks were not sys-tematically trained for their tasks in their predominantly white colleges (they had no courses, no interested professors, and did little research). Until recently, black history was not fash-ionable. One white scholar advised me as late as 1963 that I would have to discontinue my study of the black past if I wanted a future in the historical profession. This attitude was characteristic of many history departments in the country's leading graduate schools. In the 1950s when a graduate student told a professor at an Ivy League school that he wanted to write a dissertation on "Negro Thought," the professor asked, "Did they have any?" Understandably, since students at these schools could take no Negro history courses (or even obtain reading lists on the subject), had no professors who knew or cared anything about black history, and had few secondary or primary sources they could use even for self-education, they rarely wrote dissertations about blacks. The evidence of this is clear in Warren Kuehl's *Dissertations in History*. Out of the 7,635 dissertations in history completed at American colleges between 1873 and 1960, only 171 or 2.3 per cent were in any way related to blacks. One hundred and twenty-four, or 72.5 per cent of those were primarily concerned with Negroes as a problem (white attitudes toward blacks, the views of slaveholders, biographies of whites who spent a great deal of their time defending or abusing blacks, and diplomatic maneuvers of the U.S. government which involved Negroes.) Only 47 or 27.4 per cent of these dissertations concentrated on Negro life, institutions, or culture. Significantly, 17, or 36.1 per cent of these dissertations were written by Negro scholars. Surprisingly, there were more studies of white individuals and organizations that tried to oppress the Negro than there were of black communities or biographies of prominent Negroes. Traditionally, white scholars have studied the Negro only to amplify their knowledge of white men and white institutions. Although this research is essential for an understanding of American society and the place of blacks in it, it is poor preparation for those who have to teach what black men have said, done, and thought.

In spite of these limitations, many white scholars have made valuable contributions to our knowledge of the black past. In their reactions to the charges of the black students, however, some of them have overestimated their contributions. They claim that white historians, for example, have produced an overwhelming majority of the "significant" works in black history and that most of these works have appeared in the last two decades. One white historian went so far as to argue that there were *no* historians of the Negro before the 1950s. While this is partially a reflection of the intellectual arrogance which appears in each generation in regard to the one which preceded it, it also reflects a disturbing ahistorical philosophy and the intellectual arrogance of white scholars toward black scholars; black history, many whites contend, only became legitimate or significant when whites began to write about it.

Black scholars almost universally reject these arguments. They contend that white scholars have concentrated on white actors in the black historical drama, white attitudes toward blacks, and race relations. The best procedure for studying any people is rarely to focus almost exclusively on the way another group views them. More blacks have written about black institutions, individuals, and communities than white historians. (Eighty per cent of the Negro scholars who wrote dissertations on blacks between 1873 and 1960 wrote works of this type.) More of them had graduate courses in black history, generally at Negro colleges, taught by professors who were interested in and had done research in the black past than white historians did. The primary and secondary sources were located at their colleges. As a result of these factors, black scholars have produced most of the significant works in black history because they wrote about the ideas, actions, hopes, disappointments, successes, and failures of black men. In the future, as graduate training improves in white colleges, more and more white scholars will produce significant works and become qualified to teach black history.

Contrary to the arguments of many blacks, the racism of the white historian is no proof that the Negro historian is the only person who can study the black experience objectively. In light of the need of the black masses for self-pride, the Negro historian is influenced, like the white historian, by the demands of his audience. Slavery, for example, as cruel as it was, as degrading as it must have been, must be viewed by many blacks against a canvas of bondsmen rebelling at every turn. To view the institution otherwise is to foreclose the possibility that contemporary blacks, retaining, as they allegedly do, much of the slave's culture, will rise up and demand their rights.

The contention that the black historian should monopolize the teaching of the black past is a threat to his intellectual freedom. The black students argue that the experience of being white in America bars a white man from teaching "black oriented" subjects. The same reasoning, it seems to me, could be applied to blacks. If the painful experience of being black in America qualifies a black man, and him alone, to teach "black-oriented" subjects, does not that same experience bar him from teaching "white-oriented" subjects? Most whites think so. The late Malcolm X pinpointed this problem clearly: "Most whites, even when they credit a Negro with some intelligence, will still feel that all he can talk about is the race issue; most whites never feel that Negroes can contribute anything to other areas of thought, and ideas." Contemporary blacks have simply reinforced this argument. Rather than accept this view, all Negro historians must say with Frantz Fanon: "I sincerely believe that a subjective experience can be understood by others; and it would give me no pleasure to announce that the black problem is my problem and mine alone and that it is up to me to study it."

We can eliminate much of the racism which has characterized American history without bowing to all of the contemporary demands of disaffected blacks. The current movements to give more interdisciplinary training to historians will help to promote objectivity. The new emphases on comparative studies and cultural anthropology also have exciting possibilities. The best guarantee of objectivity, however, is the increasing number of Negro scholars. In their fervor to change the direction of American historiography, black scholars will shake up Clio's long and comfortable role as mistress to the white supremacist. Realizing that the black scholar is peering over his shoulder, the white historian will not be able to continue his over generalization and shoddy research on black-white relations.

While the black historians may force white historians to discard some of their racist assumptions, we must be wary of treading the path of our white supremacy predecessors in distorting history to prove a point. The contemporary insistence on the necessity for myth building and the creation of heroes is as distressing as it is unnecessary. By demanding myths many students demonstrate how vicious and how long lasting the lynching bee of the racist historians has been. It is obvious that only a people who really believe that they have done nothing of historical importance feel that they must rely so heavily on myths to build pride. Blacks must not unwittingly accept racist dogma and conclude that "objective," "factual" history can never contain anything upon which they can build pride.

Rather than trying to create myths, the black historian should seek to record the truth. He must take as his creed the following declaration of George Washington Williams, one of the first Negro historians: "Not as a blind panegyrist for my race, nor as the partisan apologist, but from the 'truth of history,' I have striven to record the truth, the whole truth, and nothing but the truth." Since he has been denied the opportunity to learn about himself, the black man needs only the facts to improve his self-image. The poet Ella Wilcox had this in mind when she wrote:

> Out of the wilderness, out of the night,
> Has the black man crawled to the dawn of light;
> He has come through the valley of great despair—
> He has borne what no white man ever can bear—
> He has come through sorrow and pain and woe,
> And the cry of his heart is to *know*, to *know!*

Mary McLeod Bethune summed up the relationship between black pride and the "truth of history" in a beautiful address to the Association for the Study of Negro Life and History in 1937:

> If our people are to fight their way up out of bondage we must arm them with the sword and the shield and the buckler of pride—belief in themselves and their possibilities, based upon a sure knowledge of the achievements of the past. . . .
>
> Through the scientific investigation and objective presentation of the facts of our history and our achievement to ourselves and to all men, . . . accurate research and investigation, we serve so to supplement, correct, re-orient and annotate the story of world progress as to enhance the standing of our group in the eyes of all men. . . .
>
> We must tell the story with continually accruing detail from the cradle to the grave. . . . As we tell this story, as we present to the world the facts, our pride in racial achievement grows, and our respect in the eyes of all men heightens.

Even when I realize that there are different kinds of truth and that the same facts can be arranged in different ways, I feel the historian should be guided by the ideals of Williams. The Negro historian who tries to build myths is a traitor not only to his profession, but also to the black masses, to the Negro's struggle for dignity, and to the black revolution. Considering all of the formidable obstacles we face in trying to bring about either meaningful integration, revolution, or separate societies, this is certainly the wrong time to swap realism for mythology. Our struggles to defeat our oppressors must be based on a dispassionate and rational analysis of the historical causes underlying our contemporary plight. Ron Karenga has stated the case perfectly: "It is better to work with hard facts than to play with pleasant but unproductive dreams." More than 30 years ago Mary Bethune saw clearly the relationship between "objective" history and black liberation. The Negro's problems, she wrote, must be described, "accurately, realistically and factually. The situation we face must be defined, reflected and evaluated. Then, armed with the pride and courage of his glorious tradition, conscious of his positive contribution to American life, and enabled to face clear-eyed and unabashed the actual situation before him, the Negro may gird his loins and go forth to battle to return 'with their shields or on them.' " Virtually the same situation prevails today. The need for realism is no less apparent. The black man has only to read the numerous accounts of the baneful effects of myths on the American white man to know how dangerous they are. The future is bleak indeed if we try to build it on evanescent mythology rather than the firm foundation of truth.

The search for truth places a heavy burden of responsibility on any historian who belongs to an oppressed group. Even while recognizing the Negro's need for increased self-respect and the contribution that history can make to this, young black scholars must be constantly aware of the relation between means and ends. Instead of becoming a propagandist, the young scholar must live up to the historical tradition created and maintained by such black men as William Wells Brown, George Washington Williams, W. E. B. Du Bois, Carter Woodson, A. A. Taylor, Charles Wesley, Rayford Logan, and John Hope Franklin. "Such a tradition," according to Charles Wesley,

> will have solid historical foundations and there must be no lack of authenticity, nor any unreliability. The traditions must have the support of documents, primary and secondary sources, and there should be no uncertainty concerning the facts. We need historians trained in the method of producing pages and pages filled with printed words, statistics and figures. At the same time, we need interpretations, portraitures, brilliant narration. There must be no mythical or legendary bases unless supported by fact. . . . Our Negro Revolution is now based upon a background of sound tradition, and it moves forward with power because of its history. . . .
>
> A people's knowledge of facts can free them from ignorance but by itself it has never inspired a crusade. The revolution needs history and it needs valued traditions. Backed by a worthy historical tradition and supported by reaffirmations of the American promise as a firm foundation, we can march forward and break the chains of public opinion which maintains contempt, derision, and second-class citizenship. On the foundation of our history, we can continue to build a lasting temple of self-respect and self-esteem, as other population groups have done.

In his efforts to record the truth, the black historian can make American history a much more worthwhile and objective subject. Because he has survived the long night of American oppression, the black man brings special skills to the task of historical analysis. First of all, barred from any share in the American dream and forced to deal with the harsh reality, the cruelty, and the brutality of American life, he is encumbered by few of the myths of American society. Second, oppressed himself, he is unlikely to take at face value the assessments of society left us by the *haves*. Instead, Negro historians will seek to obtain a hearing for the *have nots*. This will help, I think, to accelerate the current trend away from our traditional elitist approach to history. The Negro historian will also be much more skeptical than his white colleagues about the progressive improvement in American society. After all, the black experience has demonstrated the validity of the French proverb that the more things change, the more they remain the same.

When we grapple with, rather than shout about, the black studies debate, many of our problems will be solved. As black historians, we must get off of our soapbox long enough to find the evidence to support our contentions about the "correct" view of the black past. And, however laudable and necessary our debunking of Clio garbed in the raiments of white supremacy, we must concede that there may be *some* truth in the white man's view of history. At the very least, we should reject blanket condemnations of his efforts. By the same token, the white historian, regardless of his stake in the historical views built up so painfully over the years, must at least accept the right of blacks to question the legitimacy of those views.

The white historian must accept responsibility for the disrepute in which the profession stands today. He has hidden so many lies under the banner of "objectivity" that the word itself has become a synonym for falsehood among young blacks and whites. In this regard, the claim of southern historians that they have a "natural" right to teach black history is especially disturbing to most students. They argue, justifiably, that the southern historian, by his racist tracts on slavery and Reconstruction, has forfeited any "natural" right to write or teach about blacks. I am not contending that no white can write or teach about blacks. They can, I think, if they are, as Carter Woodson once said, "properly informed and have the human attitude. . . ." Whites can teach black history as long as they are willing to accept Earle Thorpe's observation that any white American can do justice to the black past,

> who is willing to be critical of his repressions and projections, and to stay on guard against the ethnic and class biases and stereotypes which abound throughout modern Occidental civilization. . . .
>
> In every area of American life, historiography *not* excepted, there has been too much *disrespect* for black people . . . anyone who hopes to integrate successfully Afro-American history must rid himself of all attitudes, ideas, and convictions of black inferiority. Also, the white teacher of black history must get rid of the notion that this history is propaganda.

White historians cannot have it both ways. They cannot claim a right to teach black history at the same time that they are spouting racist dogma. They cannot complain of the extreme lengths to which young Negro historians go to wipe out the remnants of racism in the intellectual domain while at the same time accepting all of the myths of American history themselves. Rather than rushing to the barricades to defend an allegedly chaste Clio from rape by the black historian, the white historian should examine her contemporary and past conduct to see if she may not be like a woman of easy virtue who has submitted to all willingly. Certainly, the "New Black History" should cause him to question his long and comfortably held views. The white historian should at least leave the barricades long enough to comb the sources to determine, to his own satisfaction, the validity of the contentions of the black historian. But, however disturbing his discoveries may be, they should not distort his vision. The white historian must remember that guilt is not empathy, maudlin sentimentality is not Soul, and sweeping condemnation is not truth.

The task will be easy for neither the white nor the black historian. But history has been too long embroiled in controversy for us to lose our heads in the current debate over black studies. We must not permit the current malaise to make us lose sight of those aspects of the black experience which are truly worth studying. The black experience reveals too much about the nature of American society and is too important as a subject of inquiry, for the emotionalism of a few blacks, the guilt of whites, or the indecision, fear, and bumbling of college administrators to force historians to shun their responsibility to study that experience.

We cannot rightfully complain of the charlatans, the neo-historians turned capitalists, and the hectic reprinting of worthless volumes on the black experience, if we do not produce scholarly studies of that experience. This, then, is the role of the historian in the current debate over black studies. It is our duty to provide the works, the memorial to the profession, which will remain after the contemporary generation of students have changed the universities to their liking, gone on to their life's work, or have led a successful American revolution. Finally, we should be glad that the debates between black and white historians and the demands of the black students have served to revive a subject which appeared to be on the verge of dying because of its irrelevance, or of sinking out of sight under the weight of its footnotes. The current debate may permit us, if we take advantage of the opportunity, to provide the ballast needed to steady the black studies ship as it sails through stormy seas in the years ahead.

APPENDIX

A Model Program

A Model Afro-American Studies Program: The Results of a Survey

Conducted by

JOHN W. BLASSINGAME

AMERICAN COLLEGES, forced to establish Afro-American Studies programs in a highly charged emotional atmosphere, have rarely had any guidelines to follow. All too often, scholars have been reluctant to offer constructive criticisms of the programs which have been established. It seems appropriate then, for concerned scholars to propose a model to which colleges may refer when considering the establishment of Afro-American Studies. With this in mind, in September of 1969 I drew up a draft "Model Afro-American Studies Program" and sent copies of it to 77 scholars. I attempted to obtain comments from a cross section of American scholars.

The "Model" was sent to individuals at Negro and predominantly white colleges, to sociologists, political scientists, librarians, government officials, historians, and those scholars who had written widely or taught about the black experience. The sample of scholars, of course, was not perfect; it depended primarily upon my knowledge of individuals in the field and of choosing people who had participated in scholarly meetings in the preceding two years. A little more than one-third (31) of the people who received the model, responded.

In conformity to the wishes of the respondents, I have made a number of stylistic changes in the draft. While a few of the respondents approved the general outline of the program, they dis-

Presented at the American Historical Association meeting, December 28, 1969.

agreed with specific aspects of it. Generally, the additional objectives and courses indicate the nature and extent of their disagreement. The arabic numeral in parentheses indicates the number of scholars who supported each additional objective or course.

The original draft, according to the respondents, was deficient in two areas. First, it was too parochial, focused too exclusively on the American experience. Second, the model was drawn up with predominantly white colleges in mind. Respondents from Negro colleges insisted that there should be a greater emphasis on the black student's need for pride, for improving his self-image. While Negro and predominantly white colleges will probably institute programs which differ in emphasis, it seems to me that the "Model" can serve both as a guide.

We are not suggesting that any college can or should accept this "Model" in toto. Instead, we hope that it will be used as a point of departure by colleges considering an Afro-American Studies program. We realize that local circumstances and unique needs should be the major determinants in establishing any program.

Model

The largest and most readily identifiable minority ethnic group in America, Negroes have had a profound impact on American society. No American can truly understand his own society and culture without a knowledge of the roles Negroes have played in them. It is important that American college students be given an opportunity to study a group which has formed so large a part of the population of the United States throughout its history.

Much can be learned about American life by studying the place of Negroes in American society. The American goals of freedom and equality can be more fully understood, for example, in the light of the denial of these goals to blacks and the relentless quest of both blacks and whites to fulfill them. The diversity and complexity of American society can be illuminated by studying its long history of intolerance, the reciprocal relationship between the black subculture and America's dominant western culture, and the unique historical and contemporary position of Negroes in American political, economic, social, intellectual, cultural, and artistic life.

Largely excluded from the decision-making processes and institutions, as well as from any meaningful participation in the wide spectrum of ordinary American life, Negroes cannot lay claim to having had a primary role in American society. Still, the response of blacks and whites to this exclusion is a historical and contemporary fact of prime importance. Negro slavery, the attempt to democratize a society shackled by more than 200 years of bondage, the proscription of blacks, the movement of blacks to urban centers, and Negro efforts to carve out a meaningful social, cultural, and intellectual life, have involved a great investment of time, energy, spirit, capital, blood, and suffering by Americans, black and white alike. The presence of the Negro looms so large in the American experience that it is difficult to understand that experience without a systematic examination of the place of blacks in American society. Indeed, it could be argued that one can only understand the complexity of American society by studying other multiracial societies.

Although scholars have generally made the Negro the "invisible man" of America, either through neglect or by deliberate exclusion, a rich mine of material is available for the study of black men. The literature is extensive, rich, and significant enough (see, for instance, Monroe Work's 698 page *Bibliography of the Negro* published in 1920) to justify a systematic examination of the Negro's role in American society. The intellectual works by and about black men have made a difference in American thinking about religion, music, the arts, politics, and society.

The black experience is too important to continue to be segregated out of traditional courses. Teachers of relevant courses must endeavor to make them represent the diversity of all of American life and culture. Teachers, however, have far too many other responsibilities to be expected to gain the new knowledge in their "spare time." A college's first responsibility, then, is to provide some mechanism at the departmental level (departmental seminars or lecture series) to help the faculty retool for this new responsibility. The creation of special courses on blacks in no way decreases the responsibility of teachers of many traditional courses to integrate the Negro into their syllabi (in the same way that a special course on the Civil War, or on the Frontier, does not exclude the Civil War or the Frontier from consideration in the United States history course). There is a real danger, of course, that the current enthusiasm will lead to a hydraheaded monster of new courses overlapping in content, objectives, and reading lists with little intellectual depth. Such courses are often both faulty in conception and deficient in execution. Departments must be urged to exercise restraint and to confer closely before instituting new courses.

A rigorous program in Afro-American Studies is the best way for American colleges to add another dimension to the liberally educated man who has to live in a multiracial society. Any Afro-American Studies program must serve the needs of *all* students. While we recognize the black student's desire to achieve pride, self-identity, and the means to restructure society, attainment of any of these objectives should and will be natural outgrowths of the program. All students take courses which may or may not meet their own immediate and unique needs. Similarly, each student has a special set of expectations and derives a special benefit from each course he takes. Obviously, black students, because of their experience and place in American society, will have different expectations and obtain different benefits from white students in a course on the Negro. It would seriously jeopardize the intellectual respectability of such courses, however, if they only stressed the heroic, self-glorifying nature of the black experience.

There are some social problems which are of special concern to black students to which a college may address itself outside of the

Afro-American Program. Special conferences, for example, could be arranged on racism, poverty, landlord-tenant relations in the ghetto, and welfare programs in America. Similarly, a lecture series on contemporary social problems could help black and white students to understand more clearly the nature of the society in which they live.

For the immediate future, black scholars who can teach "black" courses will be at a premium. While we reject the current mystical belief that only those with black skin can teach courses related to Negroes, it is a fact that few whites are qualified, by training, to teach these courses.

This is certainly understandable when we consider history. Before 1960 there were probably only five graduate schools in the country which offered courses in Negro history (almost all of them Negro colleges). Of course, there were many white and black scholars at other schools who developed an early interest in black studies and wrote dissertations, books, and articles on the Negro. For many the interest was ephemeral; for others peripheral; and to a few, intellectually rewarding enough to continue reading, researching, and writing long after their initial enthusiasm. At any rate, because of their more systematic training in this area, black scholars are generally better equipped, *at the moment,* to teach most black-oriented courses. Even so, the number of blacks who have obtained graduate training is small. Consequently, there are neither enough blacks nor whites to teach black-oriented courses.

Colleges will be competing in a very tight market for the limited number of people who can teach in any Afro-American Studies program. The programs cannot be inaugurated, therefore, unless the colleges provide financial support for the development of the courses to be included in them. The instructors for these courses should be supported for an entire summer and/or semester while they organize them. Concurrently, the nation's graduate schools must make a much more concerted effort to attract Negro graduate students.

We feel that a Black Studies program should be designed for all students and should fulfill the following objectives.

(23) I. Give students a clear conception of the complexity of American life.
(23) II. Acquaint students with the problems, successes, and failures of America's largest minority group.
(23) III. Enable students to lead fruitful lives in a multiracial society.

Objectives added by the respondents

(5) IV. To help students to understand the nature of contemporary racial and social turmoil and to guide them into constructive modes of thought about current issues.
(3) V. To enable students to see the black experience in a world setting.

There are, of course, several types of Black Studies programs. We would like to describe two of them briefly. The first program permits the student to pursue one of the traditional disciplines while obtaining a minor in Black Studies. Probably the best combination of courses in such a program would include the following:

(22) I. Interdisciplinary Seminar on Black Studies
(23) II. The Afro-American in United States History
(23) III. The Afro-American in American Literature
(21) IV. The Sociology of Race Relations
(21) V. Cultural Anthropology
(22) VI. Afro-American Music.

Courses added by the respondents

(7) VII. African History
(5) VIII. Politics of Race
(2) IX. The Psychology of Prejudice
(2) X. Urban Economics
(2) XI. Comparative Race Relations
(1) XII. Afro-American Family
(1) XIII. Black Thought

(I) XIV. Afro-American Drama
(I) XV. Urban Anthropology
(I) XVI. Socio-Religious Impact of the Black Church
(I) XVII. The Black Man's Psychology
(I) XVIII. History of the Middle East
(I) XIX. Economics of Racism
(I) XX. Geography of Africa
(I) XXI. History of Race Relations

The second type of Black Studies program, the departmental, should include the courses listed above and the following ones:

(22) I. Two foreign languages (French and Portuguese)
(23) II. History and Culture of Brazil
(23) III. History and Culture of the West Indies
(23) IV. American Negro Autobiographies
(22) V. Comparative Study of Slavery and Race Relations
(22) VI. Introduction to Economics
(22) VII. Introduction to Political Science
(23) VIII. African History and Culture
(23) IX. Urban Sociology
(23) X. The Negro in the City
(22) XI. Afro-American Art
(23) XII. The Impact of the Communications Media on American Society

Courses added by the respondents

(4) XIII. Spanish
(2) XIV. Latin American History
(2) XV. Religion and Racism
(2) XVI. Swahili
(I) XVII. Hausa
(I) XVIII. The World and the West: The Revolution of Modernization
(I) XIX. Comparative Study of the Development of Black Communities in the New World

(1)   XX. Afro-American and American Diplomacy
(1)   XXI. History of Afro-American Thought
(1)   XXII. Minority Groups in the American Economy
(1)   XXIII. African Art
(1)   XXIV. African Literature
(1)   XXV. Black Drama
(1)   XXVI. The Afro-American and the Third World
(1)   XXVII. Blacks and the American Political Process
(1)   XXVIII. Comparative Anthropological Study of the Afro-American in Latin America, the West Indies and the United States

The most difficult decision that most colleges have had to make is whether to establish a minor or departmental program. We cannot claim to have any solution to the problem. We would, however, like to suggest a few things which should be considered in making a decision on this matter. Emotional concern aside, each college must determine whether it has the intellectual and financial resources to inaugurate a departmental program. It would appear that many predominantly Negro colleges have the intellectual but frequently lack the financial resources to institute Black Studies departments. Many predominantly white colleges, on the other hand, have only the financial resources.

Beyond the matter of resources, each college must decide whether a department is desirable. On the one hand, all students should learn more about the black experience. But, on the other, our economic life is not specialized enough yet to offer many employment opportunities to specialists in Afro-American studies.

As far as black students are concerned, the losses inherent in majoring in Black Studies may outweigh the gains. Although Negroes certainly need to know more about themselves, their greatest need is to learn more about the multitude of subjects offered at American universities. Whether Negroes want to participate more fully in American society, or separate entirely from it, they are in dire need of more black scientists, doctors, economists, engineers, communications experts, architects, writers, linguists, lawyers, and historians. We cannot produce these if all black students major in Black Studies. We can, on the other hand, produce these and others, if blacks are given the opportunity to learn about themselves in a minor, rather than a departmental program.

We realize that a departmental program open to all students does not carry any inherent proscription against blacks majoring in other subjects. Given the current emotion-charged atmosphere on our campuses, however, we are afraid that social pressure will force a number of Negro students into the program in spite of their real interest in other subjects.

Predominantly Negro colleges have had so much experience in so many of the areas that are now causing ferment in American higher education, that they can play a vital role in helping to shape the direction of many movements connected with Black Studies. First, they can advise predominantly white colleges on the best ways to change their antiquated admissions procedures. Second, they can advise predominantly white colleges on the best community action programs to adopt and the best ways to help poorly prepared students to succeed in college. Third, since they have had so much more experience at integrating material on the Negro into college courses, they can advise predominantly white colleges wishing to establish Black Studies programs. All of these efforts should involve the establishment of consortia, faculty exchange programs, and faculty institutes arranged by the Negro colleges. To the harried black dean, such programs may help him to halt the black brain drain.

Cooperative efforts between predominantly white and predominantly Negro colleges are especially desirable if the nation's library facilities are to be used rationally. While we applaud the efforts of many colleges to encourage their students to do research on the Negro, we realize that the Negro college libraries, where most of the source material is located, are woefully understaffed. In fact, these libraries are so understaffed that they may have to close their doors to the horde of scholars and students descending on them from across the country. If we are to tap the rich mine of material on the Negro in these libraries in the next few years, regional and national associations of predominantly while colleges must provide the funds for the expansion of staffs and facilities at these libraries.

Respondents

Irving H. Bartlett
Carnegie Mellon University

David W. Bishop
Fayetteville State College

William Brewer, Editor
Journal of Negro History

William Brown
Yale University

Lawrence C. Bryant
South Carolina State College

Joel Colton
Duke University

Philip Curtin
University of Wisconsin

Philip S. Foner
Lincoln (Pa.) University

Eugene Genovese
University of Rochester

William Gibson
Sacramento State College

Noel Gray
Southern University (La.)

Sarah Jackson
National Historical Publications
Commission

Alandus Johnson
Paine College (Ga.)

Eugene Levy
Carnegie Mellon University

W. F. Low
University of Maryland
(Baltimore)

James McPherson
Princeton University

Paul McStallworth
Central State College

August Meier
Kent State University

Edwin Redkey
University of Tennessee

Joe M. Richardson
University of Florida

Willie Lee Rose
University of Virginia

Elliott Rudwick
Kent State University

Alonzo T. Stephens
Tennessee State University

Earle E. Thorpe
North Carolina Central College

George B. Tindall
University of North Carolina

Hanes Walton
Savannah State College

Charles H. Wesley
Executive Director
Association for the Study of
Negro Life and History

Chancellor Williams
Howard University

Robin Winks
Yale University

Charles E. Wynes
University of Georgia

Selected Bibliography

Blassingame, John W. " 'Soul' or Scholarship: Choices Ahead for Black Studies." *Smithsonian* I (April, 1970): 58–65.

Brimmer, Andrew. "The Black Revolution and the Economic Future of Negroes in the United States." *American Scholar* XXXVIII (Autumn, 1969): 629–43.

Bunzell, John H. "Black Studies at San Francisco State." *Public Interest,* Fall, 1968, pp. 22–38.

Chew, Peter. "Black History, or Black Mythology?" *American Heritage* XX (August, 1969): 4–9.

Clarke, Austin C. "Cultural-Political Origins of Black Student Anti-Intellectualism." *Studies in Black Literature* I (Spring, 1970): 69–82.

Cleaver, Eldridge. "Education and Revolution." *Black Scholar* I (November, 1969): 44–52.

Cleveland, B. "Black Studies and Higher Education." *Phi Delta Kappan* LI (September, 1969): 44 46.

Coles, Flournoy. "Black Studies in the College Curriculum." *Negro Educational Review* XX (October, 1969): 106–13.

Curl, Charles H. "Black Studies: Form and Content." *CLA Journal* XIII (September, 1969): 1–9.

Dillon, Merton L. "White Faces and Black Studies." *Commonweal* XCI (January 30, 1970): 476–79.

Drimmer, Melvin. "Teaching Black History in America: What Are the Problems?" *Negro History Bulletin* XXXIII (February, 1970): 32–34.

Dunbar, Ernest. "Cornell: The Black Studies Thing." *New York Times Magazine,* April 6, 1969, p. 25.

Durley, G. L. "Center for Black Students on University Campuses." *Journal of Higher Education* XL (June, 1969): 473–76.

Easum, Donald B. "The Call for Black Studies." *Africa Report* XIV (May–June, 1969): 16–22.

Furniss, W. T. "Racial Minorities and Curriculum Change." *Educational Record* L (Fall, 1969): 360–70.

Gibson, E. F. "Three D's: Distortion, Deletion, Denial." *Social Education* XXXIII (April, 1969): 405–9.

Hamilton, Charles V. "The Question of Black Studies." *Phi Delta Kappan* LI (March, 1970): 365–68.

Harding, Vincent. "Achieving Educational Equality: Stemming the Black Brain Drain." *Current* CV (March, 1969): 37–40.

Harding, Vincent. "Black Students and the 'Impossible' Revolution." *Ebony* XXIV (August, 1969): 141–49.

Harding, Vincent. "Beyond Chaos: Black History and the Search for the New Land." *Amistad* 1: 267–92.

Hatch, John. "Black Studies: The Real Issue." *Nation* CCVIII (June 16, 1969): 755–58.

Henshel, A. M., and Henshel, R. L. "Black Studies Programs: Promise and Pitfalls." *Journal of Negro Education* XXXVIII (Fall, 1969): 423–29.

Poinsett, A. "Think Tank for Black Scholars." *Ebony* XXV (February, 1970): 46–48.

Poussaint, Alvin, and Atkinson, Carolyn. "Black Youth and Motivation." *Black Scholar* I (March, 1970): 43–51.

Redding, Saunders. "The Black Youth Movement." *American Scholar* XXVIII (Autumn, 1969): 584–87.

Roberts, S. V. "Black Studies: More Than Soul Courses." *Commonweal* XCI (January 30, 1970): 478–79.

Robinson, Armstead L., Foster, Craig C., and Ogilvie, Donald H., eds. *Black Studies in the University*. New Haven, 1969.

Rosovsky, H. "Black Studies at Harvard: Personal Reflections Concerning Recent Events." *American Scholar* XXXVIII (Autumn, 1969): 562–72.

Rousseve, Ronald J. "Dealing Responsibly with the Black American." *Negro Educational Review* XX (October, 1969): 95–105.

Rustin, Bayard, ed. *Black Studies: Myths and Realities*. New York, 1969.

"Student Strikes: 1968–69." *Black Scholar* I (January–February, 1970): 65–75.

Vontress, Clemmont E. "Black Studies—Boon or Bane?" *Journal of Negro Education* XXXIX (Summer, 1970): 192–201.

Warr, J. "Black History and Culture." *NCEA Bulletin* LXV (May, 1969): 51–55.

Wilson, C. E. "Case for Black Studies." *Educational Leadership* XXVII (December, 1969): 218–21.

Woodward, C. Vann. "Clio with Soul." *The Journal of American History* LVI (June, 1969): 5–20.

Wright, Stephen J. "Black Studies and Sound Scholarship." *Phi Delta Kappan* LI (March, 1970): 365–68.